DIPLOMACY
IN
MODERN EUROPEAN HISTORY

MAIN THEMES IN EUROPEAN HISTORY

Bruce Mazlish, General Editor

DIPLOMACY

IN

MODERN EUROPEAN HISTORY

Edited by

LAURENCE W. MARTIN

Wilson Professor of International Politics
University of Wales

THE MACMILLAN COMPANY, NEW YORK
COLLIER-MACMILLAN LIMITED, LONDON

THE MACMILLAN COMPANY, NEW YORK
COLLIER-MACMILLAN CANADA, LTD., TORONTO, ONTARIO

PRINTED IN THE UNITED STATES OF AMERICA

FOREWORD

History, we are frequently told, is a seamless web. However, by isolating and studying the strands that compose the tapestry of man's past, we are able to discern the pattern, or patterns, of which it is comprised. Such an effort does not preclude a grasp of the warp and woof, and the interplay of the strands; rather, it eventually demands and facilitates such a comprehension. It is with this in mind that the individual volumes of the MAIN THEMES series have been conceived.

The student will discover, for example, that the population changes discussed in one volume relate to the changes in technology traced in another volume; that both changes are affected by, and affect in turn, religious and intellectual developments; and that all of these changes and many more ramify into a complicated historical network through all the volumes. In following through this complex interrelationship of the parts, the student recreates for himself the unity of history.

Each volume achieves its purpose, and its appeal to a general audience, by presenting the best articles by experts in the field of history and allied disciplines. In a number of cases, the articles have been translated into English for the first time. The individual volume editor has linked these contributions into an integrated account of his theme, and supplied a selected bibliography by means of footnotes for the student who wishes to pursue the topic further. The introduction is an original treatment of the problems in the particular field. It provides continuity and background for the articles, points out gaps in the existing literature, offers new interpretations, and suggests further research.

The volumes in this series afford the student of history an unusual opportunity to explore subjects either not treated, or touched upon lightly in a survey text. Some examples are population—the dramatis personae of history; war—the way of waging peace by other means; the rise of technology and science in relation to society; the role of religious and cultural ideas and institutions; the continuous ebb and flow of exploration and colonialism; and the political and economic works contrived by modern man. Holding fast to these Ariadne threads, the student penetrates the fascinating labyrinth of history.

BRUCE MAZLISH, *General Editor*

CONTENTS

INTRODUCTION

The word diplomacy in the title of this volume is used not in its narrower sense of the professional work of a diplomat, but in its wider reference to the full range of international politics [1] as in the familiar phrase 'diplomatic history.' Yet this is certainly not an attempt to compile an excessively condensed diplomatic history of Europe. Rather it is an effort to suggest how diplomatic history can be used to enquire into the fundamental characteristics of the modern international system and to illuminate the processes by which it has evolved.

Relatively few writers have tried to look closely and consistently at the essential characteristics of the interstate system as distinct from the details of its periodic manifestations.[2] Such efforts are not without their perils. One may succeed only in replacing the possibly narrow view of the conventional diplomatic histories with generalizations so abstract as to be meaningless. Worse, there may arise a temptation to read into historical periods such characteristics as will serve arbitrary theories of continuity or change. These perils are the greater because consideration of the evolutionary processes of history, and particularly international history, with its issues of peace and war, frequently brings out the polemical urge in observers who see in interpretations of the past the possible source of solutions for the problems of the present.

This in itself is one of the most cogent arguments for encouraging methodical and careful studies of the international system, for some interpretation of its development, even if unacknowledged, underlies the work of all historians and contemporary publicists. We should not, however, expect to arrive at an easy consensus on the subject. Historians differ sharply even as to what the characteristics of a particular diplomatic era were, let alone as to which of those characteristics should be

[1] The writings of Sir Harold Nicolson form the most widely accepted introduction to the study of diplomacy in the narrower sense of technique: particularly his *Diplomacy* (London: Home University Library, 1939), and his *The Evolution of Diplomatic Method* (London: Constable, 1954).

[2] Two recent ventures into this field, both represented in this volume, are F. H. Hinsley, *Power and the Pursuit of Peace: Theory and Practice in the History of Relations Between States* (Cambridge: Cambridge University Press, 1963), and Richard N. Rosecrance, *Action and Reaction in World Politics: International Systems in Perspective* (Boston: Little, Brown, 1963). See also Stanley Hoffmann (ed.), *Contemporary Theory in International Relations* (Englewood Cliffs, N. J.: Prentice-Hall, 1960), and G. Liska, *International Equilibrium* (Cambridge, Mass.: Harvard University Press, 1957).

regarded as essential or as to what were the processes of change and transition. The readings and comments that follow can consequently only be regarded as a suggested introduction to the task of applying the reader's own historical knowledge to the broader questions raised.

It will be seen that a certain consistency of interpretation can be extracted from the writing that follows, but this is far from being the only conceivable interpretation or even from being one to which all the authors represented would subscribe. There are those, for example, who emphasise change in the history of the international system. Of these some see steady progress toward order; others a constantly rising curve of destructiveness. For others the system has been cyclic, periods of order interspersed with periods of disruption. In a sense all such interpretations can be arbitrary, depending on the way in which one chooses to define terms and compare phenomena. The extracts provided here, however, can be regarded as offering a powerful case for considering continuity during the period under discussion as more impressive than change: continuity in which the leading characteristics are the multipolar nature of the system, a common acceptance of this as a natural order, and the maintenance of the system by a structure of countervailing power, never coherently organized but never wholly escaping some bounds of restraint.

Modern European diplomacy is, of course, the ancestor of contemporary world politics. The European model of the state has become universal and the European pattern of international relations has consequently extended everywhere. From this point of view the world is Europe writ large and the peoples of other regions have made hardly the most marginal modifications to the system. There are two reasons why the present is a highly appropriate time to reflect upon the nature and development of this system, one incontrovertible, one highly controversial. Indubitable is the fact that for most of its history the European system existed in isolation while the rest of the world served only for the projection of European concerns. Now the world is an active generator of policy and Europe is at most a typical part of a larger whole. A purely European diplomatic system must therefore be regarded as a closed period of history.

Much more controversial is the suggestion that this extension has taken place at the same time as economic and technological developments have outmoded the European style of international relations. According to this argument, it is not merely the closed European system that is vanishing but the diplomatic system itself as known for the last three or four centuries.

The features suggested as characteristic of the European state system—a multiplicity of units, several of comparable size, claiming the full allegiance of citizens, vying incessantly with each other for power but fully accepting such pluralism as the proper order of things rather than harking back or looking forward to a hierarchical organization of the whole—first emerged in modern Europe among the city states of Italy. It is this process of emergence that Garrett Mattingly eloquently depicts in 'The Italian Beginnings of Modern Diplomacy.' As he points out, such beginnings cannot be neatly ascribed to a particular moment; the old and the new coexist and before the old features are entirely erased, still newer ones emerge. In particular, doctrine commonly lags behind practice. Thus it was to be some two hundred years in Europe at large before the concept of Europe organized as a single unit was finally abandoned.

Yet, as Mattingly shows, the Italian city states did, over a period, develop many of the characteristics and much of the frame of mind that go with the later interstate system. Negotiation, alliance, and even balance of power can be discerned at many levels of human relations. The achievement of the city states was to make the state the paramount vehicle for such activities and to create a clear-cut distinction between politics within the states, which were hierarchical, and politics between the states, which were egalitarian and governed not by authority but by equilibrium.

As a result of proximity and accessibility to each other's power the city states developed the struggle for power to perhaps a higher degree of intensity than the states of Europe at large were able to achieve for three or four centuries. Mattingly illustrates the reciprocal relationship between this struggle and the internal development of the state. War was both the imperative and the justification for a more and more intensive mobilization of the state's resources. The multiple allegiances of feudal and religious political structures were replaced by single allegiance to the supreme vehicle of external security. Along with the development of these powerful political machines and the corresponding relationships of struggle and balance between them went the elaboration of the techniques for precise and rational communication between them. Thus this is also the seminal period for the techniques of modern diplomacy in the narrower professional sense. Again this external development was closely related to the domestic rise of a middle class that alone could provide the skill and application necessary for the bureaucratic organization of internal energies and external relations.

Yet it would be safest to regard the Italian state system as an analogy and portent of the later European version. The scale of Italian politics was so small and so personal that the Italian rivalries were more intense, threats more total, and conflict more completely absorbing of the states' energies than those of their European successors. The city state system was more a caricature of the modern state system than an actual example of it on a small scale.

The emergence of the great European states in the seventeenth century gave rise to a multistate system on a continental scale. This system grew in both intensity and extent as the new state increased its competence to sustain policy and as communications and economic activity expanded. At one and the same time Europeans experienced a new sense of diversity and a heightened appreciation that the energetic dialectical relationships of the new political units constituted a common and truly European system. As Sir George Clark suggests in his chapter on Europe in the seventeenth century, this was the period in which the idea that the proper political organization for Europe was an integrated structure like the Empire was replaced by a conscious appreciation of a system of multiple units holding each other in mutual restraint. The doctrine of the balance of power was now articulated more clearly than ever before as the fitting formula for such a system. The Treaty of Westphalia (1648) explicitly recognised the existence of separate sovereignties in which rulers, people, and territory formed a unity to replace the overlapping loyalties of the feudal type. Hence it also recognised a society of states. Later, the Treaty of Utrecht (1713), while still alluding to the concept of an integral 'Christendom,' was the first general settlement of Europe designed avowedly to preserve the balance of power.

The articulation of a principle must not be confused with the invention of a practice. Balance-of-power policies have been pursued in all ages and in many walks of life. But in the seventeenth century the balance of power was recognised as the conscious spirit of modern diplomacy. For the previous two centuries a structure of multiple sovereign units had been emerging under the shadow of a concept of Empire to which successive contenders like Spain and France had aspired. In its early articulations the balance-of-power concept suggested the need for would-be sovereign states to resist the current aspirant to hegemony. So successful were these policies that after the defeat of Louis XIV no immediate new contender appeared. The balance of power came to be regarded not as the way in which a system of multiple sovereignties might emerge but as the principle upon which the system indeed operated. Hope that a would-be hegemonial power could be restrained was replaced by confidence that it could.

The increasing competence of the state and range of its contacts bred a corresponding elaboration of procedures for both conflict and collaboration. Clark describes the proliferation of diplomatic techniques, now on a continental scale, the professionalization of the machinery for executing foreign policy and the invention of the congress or conference as an appropriate multilateral device for the conduct of major matters in a world of increasingly well-defined multiple sovereignties.

By drawing attention to these devices to ensure that the ever-growing power of the state was exercised externally in a controlled fashion, and by describing the parallel growth of international law, Clark compels recognition of the often denied truth that the restraints imposed by the multistate system upon the unfettered self-assertion of any of its members entitle it to be regarded as a source of order rather than disorder. Admittedly it is a system that many find unsatisfactory and for which they feel there must be a preferable alternative. Clark himself implies as much when he observes that the diplomacy of the seventeenth century 'had in it very little of a rational attempt to manage the world's affairs for the general advantage.' [3] The period of transition from the seventeenth to the eighteenth century, when consciousness of the emerging pattern was still accompanied by a vivid conception of the supposed medieval unity it was replacing, affords a context in which to ponder the merits of the multistate system as it should be debated, against the background of a concrete alternative.

For one should not exaggerate the modernity of the seventeenth century. There were still strong reminders of the old European idea. Even the impresarios of emergent international law saw it as a law between the various territories of a single jurisdiction rather than in the later form of an empirical description of the norms actually observed by sovereign entities. The career of Louis XIV illustrates the transitional nature of the age, for while the style of his ambitions showed that a prince could still aspire to universal empire, the manner of his defeat and terms of the treaties that terminated his efforts demonstrated that they were not only vain but old-fashioned.

The decades of warfare that marked the turning of the seventeenth century had produced a rapid acceleration in the development of the state and its external relations. Warfare and the progress of domestic organization continued hand in hand to make the one more strenuous

[3] See below, p. 29.

and the other more efficient. Centralized bureaucratic administration strode forward in the more advanced states to achieve unprecedented standards of finance and management. The prospering of a mercantile middle class facilitated the professionalization of wider areas of state endeavour, as it had once done on a smaller scale in the Italian context.

These improvements were naturally reflected in international affairs. Professionalization extended to the conduct of peaceful diplomacy and of war. Foreign offices with considerable staffs and archives were established, along with the first considerable standing armies since Roman times. These were supported by a new scale of logistical effort, the burdens of which provided additional incentive to increase the efficiency with which the state's resources were mobilized.

The achievement of a higher order of power for the state coincided with the appearance of new states of European consequence. Conquests in campaigns against the Turks raised Austria to a level where she could compete with a France chastened by defeat. England was released from her civil disorders to play a renewed part in diplomacy. Military ambitions stimulated Russia to modernize herself, and Prussia, also moved in large part by military considerations, solidified her dominions into a power of a respectable if not of the first rank.

Multiplication of the powers rendered the hegemony of any one less plausible. Paradoxically, as rulers became more powerful in absolute terms than ever before, their chances of becoming all powerful in Europe declined; for international power is measured not absolutely but at the margin of advantage over opponents. The emergence of the familiar European Great Powers, several in number and comparable in strength, thus created what many regard as the classic conditions for a stable balance of power. Be that as it may, the Great Powers that then appeared all survived as the leading features of world politics until well into the twentieth century.

The eighteenth century was thus the world's first experience of politics among the Great Powers. As a result, the experience of this century has deeply colored all subsequent diagnoses of the international system. Unfortunately there is no unanimous interpretation of the eighteenth-century experience. Many commentators have seen the period as one of limited conflict and ordered stability, sustained by nicely judged shifts in alignment and a rare degree of political skill. The century has thus become a revered symbol for the many who would advocate some form of limited war or traditionalist diplomacy for the present day. There is a contrary view, however, which holds that the orderliness was an illusion and the preoccupation with shifting alliances and balance of power the cause of constant war and unrest.

In his succinct discussion of most of the arguments usually adduced in this controversy, Richard Rosecrance probably represents the majority view in depicting the period as one of unusual moderation. This he attributes in part to ideological, in part to technical, factors. The absence of national enthusiasm and the cosmopolitanism of elites resulted in ambitions that fell short of extreme demands on other states and gave rulers freedom from popular compulsion to pursue their policies to excess. No ideological inhibitions prevented shifts of alignment to preserve the balance. At the same time, inefficiency in the mobilization of resources and the crude nature of military forces led to a conservative attitude toward the expenditure of armed power and precluded any hope of annihilating an enemy. Hence for Rosecrance 'the eighteenth century met the requirement for a balance of power mechanism in all these ways and the maxims of the balance of power theory were obeyed as never before or since. . . . As long as limited war held sway the balance system could not be undermined by a single Power.'[4]

There is much to be said for this opinion, but it can be overdrawn. The degree of violence was really quite substantial and the flexibility of the alliance system rather less than Rosecrance implies. It is certainly true that military forces were weak compared to those of later periods and that ideological enthusiams were less powerful and restrictive than in the years before or since. But nevertheless states were persistent and ruthless in pursuit of their ambitions against each other. There is therefore some reason to believe that Rosecrance is on firmer ground when he attributes such stability and moderation as the eighteenth century displayed to the configuration of the system, and particularly the equality of contenders, than when he cites their internal nature or the quality of their tools.[5]

No one could deny that the physical capacity of weapons affects what can be achieved or that the nature of certain weapons may, as in our own time, go some way to dictate the mode of their employment. Yet any weapon system, be it minimal or excessive in intrinsic destructiveness, may be a tolerably effective instrument of policy in the absence of substantial opposition. It seems reasonable to suggest that what limited the contests of the eighteenth century was not the capacity to

[4] See below p, 39.
[5] Cf. George Liska's perceptive article, 'Continuity and Change in International Systems,' *World Politics* **XVI** (1963–64), pp. 118–36.

nurse ambition—which seems to have been high—or to mobilize resources or administer territory—which, if not great, was much greater than before—but the fact that these capacities were distributed in such a way as to create a balance of countervailing power, the only reliable regulator among sovereign actors. According to this analysis limited war would be the result rather than the condition for a balance of power, and moderation the result of frustration rather than goodwill.

By fostering the already emergent element of mass enthusiasm that we have come to call nationalism, the French Revolution, and the subsequent wars, injected new ambitions into international politics and offered new opportunities for mobilizing the resources of the state. It is easy to exaggerate the pace of this development but the early years of the nineteenth century undoubtedly experienced the rise of a new consciousness of national identity. But while this may have generated new issues and new rigidities of outlook, it is not clear that it occasioned any changes in the outward behavior of states so fundamental as to revolutionize the pattern of their dealings.[6]

After the Napoleonic wars, advances in the destructive potential of states were followed by further development of the machinery for conducting their peaceable dealings. The full-fledged congress experiment, with its overtones of an effort to transcend the system of sovereignties, subsided into the constellation described by F. H. Hinsley in his chapter on 'The Concert of Europe.' This was an elaboration of the machinery available to carry on the traditional relations of states in an age of improved communication and altogether more intense economic and social activity. As a vehicle for the legitimization of such arrangements as proved tolerable to the Great Powers, the concert was a distinct addition to the supports of international harmony. In its earlier years, as so often after major wars and settlements, a relative consensus upon the status quo among the powerful made the potentialities of concert management seem greater than they intrinsically were. This happy state of affairs was further sustained by the accident that Great Britain, the state most in the ascendant, was peculiarly inhibited by geography, tradition, and opportunity elsewhere from fully exploiting the margin of superiority it might have enjoyed in Europe.

But the harmony within the concert was the result of a balance among the powers, not the cause. As Hinsley puts it, 'their acceptance

---

[6] From the vast literature on nationalism one might select Hans Kohn, *The Idea of Nationalism* (New York: Macmillan, 1944); Karl W. Deutsch, *Nationalism and Social Communication* (New York: John Wiley & Sons for Technology Press, M. I. T., 1953).

of the restraints and frustrations of the Concert system was the consequence rather than the cause of their preparedness to be restrained
. . . each was deterred from too much risk alone by the lack of preponderant power.' [7] When political shifts, economic development, and
technological advances upset the countervailing balance of power, vast
opportunities were presented to leaders who proved fully capable of
pursuing them. The result was upheaval culminating in the Bismarckian
conquests.

Imperial Germany constituted a new unit not easily fitted into the
balance. Bismarck's cautious balancing policy after 1871 made it
unnecessary to deal with the new preponderance immediately. But
this was the moderation of a man and not, as in the British case, of
a preponderant nation distracted by other concerns and partially iso-
lated by special circumstances. Germany's conceivable diplomatic ambitions were disruptive ones. Bismarck's own conquests had nurtured
disturbing resentments and publicized the potential of new military
methods based upon modern industry. His removal heralded a search
for a new equilibrium upon a new scale of power.

Mobilization of material power now reached dimensions out of all
proportion to preceding achievements. Europe entered upon a military
course leading directly to the developments of our own day that are
so widely believed to render obsolescent all traditional methods of
preserving the state.

The first fully ripened fruit of this process was the Great War of
1914–1918, the roots of which are explored by Raymond Aron in his
chapter on total war. Military technology was on the way to becoming
a self-generating force. Weaponry dictated, or was believed to dictate,
first, strategy and, then, diplomacy. That the war was a prolonged dead-
lock may conceivably have been an accidental result of Germany's
defeat on the Marne. But the moral and material potential existed for
massive, sustained destruction and for resilience in the face of that
destruction. In this case, symmetry of power, which if duly appreci-
ated can breed restraint, led, perhaps because of miscalculation, to
excess. Aron well depicts the interaction of psychological and physical
forces to produce a war total in methods, in ends, and in the degree to
which the momentum of the struggle escaped the capacity of statesmen
to control or even foresee. The all-out employment of national resources to mount the greatest possible destructive effort might succeed
in simply averting defeat in a technical sense, but it began to appear
too clumsy an instrument for any more subtle purpose.

[7] See below, p. 51.

The catastrophe bred further conscious efforts to modify the workings of the international system. As in the early days of the concert, there was some ambiguity as to whether the purpose was to transform the system or merely enable it to work better. Certainly the practical effects of the League experiment were no more than to provide a new framework within which the traditional balancing processes might work. A lingering belief in some minds—particularly in what we are told to consider the Anglo-Saxon countries—that it was desirable to reject the notion of countervailing power entirely, combined with war weariness, dissension among the victors, and simple ineptitude to inhibit the status quo powers from playing their proper countervailing role. The result was a disastrously slow reaction to the challenge of the totalitarian powers whose policies and methods are discussed by Gordon Craig.

In this essay Craig offers a sharp vignette of the peculiar climate of the interwar years of crisis, years that on first sight appear untypical but which, on closer examination, prove to exemplify many of the principles of traditional statecraft.

Fascist Italy, Craig demonstrates, was largely bluster and secured her very limited successes mainly as a result of the miscalculations and indifference of her distracted opponents. Nazi Germany was an altogether more serious player, mobilizing considerable power and carrying a ruthless policy to extreme lengths. Yet in many respects Nazi Germany falls comfortably within the traditional outlines of an expansionist state and, indeed, in many ways showed a higher degree of conformity to the principles of conduct required for successful operation in the international system than did her opponents. Hitler exploited with immense skill the full classic repertoire of maneuver and alignment to pick his way through the configurations of power to his goal. Despite the aura of militarism that attached to his regime, he was far from relying upon brute force in total preference to manipulating the diplomatic balances. Armed force was one instrument in his orchestra of diplomatic means. Nor did Hitler's ambitions imply a rejection rather than a rearrangement of the state system. It is in such respects that one can perhaps most readily concede the valid element in A. J. P. Taylor's recent controversial judgment that Hitler's international policies did not go beyond those to be expected of a traditional German statesman.

Even if one were to concede that Hitler's motives and those of his entourage went beyond normal experience, the problem he presented to his foes was a largely traditional one of containing an ambitious power. Much the same could be said of Bolshevik Russia. Here, it is true, was a force which, if able to implement its full original ideological purposes, would have recast the political system of the world. But it is dubious whether this ambition could have been realized even in the absence of opposition. Certainly, in the actual political environment, the Communists rapidly took on, as Craig shows, not merely a conventional concern for national interest but much of the traditional style of diplomacy. Admittedly Communists bring to international politics characteristic attitudes and assumptions from their own doctrine and from a vivid appreciation of their own conspiratorial past.[8] But beyond the refinement of some special techniques in the margins between peace and war, the Communists have not succeeded in transforming world politics into something other than a confrontation of states. The fragmentation of their own bloc now raises the possibility that they will recognise this not merely in practice but in doctrine.

The ultimate collision between the Fascist dictators and their enemies was the first true world war, when measured by the full-fledged participation of the extra-European powers in a conflict that was only partially European in its origins and issues. Europe's pattern of inter-state politics was now spread worldwide. A simultaneous geometrical increase in technological potential has, however, led many to conclude that the state system has been transformed at the same time as it has been transferred. Modern weapons of mass destruction in particular have been credited with rendering the state wholly permeable to external power and hence incapable of performing its prime function of protecting the lives and interests of its inhabitants.[9]

If the unit loses its characteristic quality, then the nature of the system must also be expected to change. Many observers therefore expect to see or already claim to discern fundamental changes in the world order: perhaps in the direction of hierarchical organization on a universal or regional scale, perhaps merely in the abandonment by states of their military force as a method of self-defence, a change from which further transformations would swiftly follow even if their exact nature cannot be foreseen.

Yet upon rigorous examination the evidence that the contemporary world political system is departing radically from the model provided by modern Europe is unconvincing. So far as the new universalistic device of the United Nations is concerned, Inis Claude makes it

[8] An interesting discussion of this occurs in Nathan Leites, *A Study of Bolshevism* (Glencoe, Ill.: The Free Press, 1953).

[9] For an expression of this view, see John H. Herz, 'Rise and Demise of the Territorial State,' *World Politics* **XI** (1956–57), pp. 473–93.

abundantly clear that continuity is more apparent than change. Looking at the United Nations as a reflection of the organization of power in the world, the common perspective of all the writings presented here, Claude ably demonstrates that the effects have been at most a marginal modification of the classic balance of power. Once again, he shows, what was regarded by many as an essay in transforming the multistate system has in practice merely provided an additional framework within which the balance of countervailing power can seek equilibrium.

This is neither more nor less than one would expect, for, as Claude points out in a perceptive sentence, 'the balance of power system, involving the freedom and responsibility of states to look to their own position within the international configuration of power, does not have to be adopted; it exists, until and unless an alternative arrangement for managing the power relationships of states is put into effect.' [10] No such alternative has been discovered. What has emerged, Claude suggests, is a more or less stable and cautious balance of power developing as experience has taught the powers that in this generation there are few easy gains to be won. This has moderated conflict and even encouraged some use of the new diplomatic devices in a form of preventive diplomacy to arrest contests for which the participants can foresee no advantageous outcome. Rather than a revolution in world affairs, this is a confirmation of the happier elements in what has gone before. 'The potential contribution of the United Nations in our times,' concludes Claude, lies 'in helping to improve and stabilize the working of the balance of power system.' [11]

Similarly cautious conclusions are suggested by a calmer look at the implications of allegedly revolutionary technology. As Michael Howard points out, in one of the few discussions of modern military affairs set in an adequate historical context, the unprecedented physical power of modern weapons may not necessarily have transformed the task of achieving political ends with them. Well before the advent of nuclear weapons, modern technology had begun to let warfare get wholly out of hand as an instrument of policy. Pursued on a modern scale, the task of eliminating the enemy's power to make war becomes self-defeating. But a growing reluctance to engage in total war does not necessarily imply inability to use military power at all. It merely calls for new techniques of management. As Howard observes, 'Those who wish to use violence as an instrument of policy—and since 1945 they have not been rare—can find, as did Hitler, more limited and

[10] See below, p. 101.
[11] See below, p. 109.

effective forms; and those who hope to counter it need equally effective instruments for doing so.' [12]

Thus recent developments are producing major changes in military affairs but it seems unlikely that these will render states incapable of continuing to struggle with each other in a violent way, still less that they will bring about the demise of the state. It is employable power that counts and the balance of destructiveness that inhibits full use of military power preserves much more of the multilateral nature of international affairs than the discrepancy between the material resources of the superpowers and the remaining states would otherwise lead one to expect. States are not permeable to weapons that no one dare use. None of this is to deny that if strategy is not successfully adapted and modern weapons are used in old ways, the results would indeed be catastrophic. But it is a foolhardy observer who would venture to predict what the complexion of the diplomatic world would be after such an upheaval.

It remains to return briefly to Europe itself to consider whether in the changing circumstances of our day the old continent may be abandoning in its own affairs the multistate system it has bequeathed to the world. Unmistakably major changes in the pattern of relationships between states in the western part of the continent have made it impossible to shirk the question raised by Stephen Graubard as to whether there is a 'new Europe.' Disillusionment in many parts of Europe as to whether the old states can any longer serve the economic, political, and military needs of their inhabitants has combined with the pressures of the superpowers and an almost complete abandonment of the idea that military action against each other would serve any useful purpose, to encourage much experimentation with new forms of organization. If this were to lead to full-blooded federal union, there would be no reason to regard this as the precursor of a similar worldwide movement to outmode international politics altogether. It would, however, eliminate this traditional system from the area of union.

What the future of this potentially federal area will actually be remains obscure. It is no longer possible to share the confidence felt by many in the late fifties that a federal *dénouement* was imminent. Military action among the West Europeans seems a remote possibility, but with that major exception the maneuverings and pressures among the various European powers still have the familiar aspect of international politics such as the continent has known for centuries.

Graubard suggests that what the Europeans seek is not so much

[12] See below, p. 116.

to transform the international system as to find an appropriate place for themselves within it. It must be left to time to determine whether they will do so as a new unity or, as now seems likely, by designing a revived and reinvigorated role for the old established states, strengthened but not eliminated by novel forms of cooperation among themselves.

Even if one of the tighter forms of unity should be realized in Western Europe, it would dispose of only a part of the old European system. Traditional diplomacy between sovereign powers will continue into the foreseeable future as the political pattern of the old continent. All the more is this true of the wider world upon which the European style has been imposed. Neither technological nor political developments would seem to have transformed the most essential characteristics of the system of interstate relations that began to emerge in Europe in the fifteenth century and attained a classic form in the eighteenth.

Unquestionably the scale of operations has extended greatly and the means available to states have become much more powerful in themselves. But the record presented to the reader in the chapters that follow suggests that there has been no fundamental alteration in the essential qualities of the system itself as one in which a multiplicity of units, relying upon selfhelp for their own preservation, preserve the system by maintaining a shifting but adequate equilibrium among themselves. The period of diplomatic history that began to open some five hundred years ago has not yet been vouchsafed a clear glimpse of its successor however wistfully some prophets may anticipate its coming.

LAURENCE W. MARTIN
Aberystwyth, Wales

THE ITALIAN BEGINNINGS OF
MODERN DIPLOMACY *

Garrett Mattingly

Garrett Mattingly was Professor of European History at Columbia University and an authority on Anglo-Spanish relations in the sixteenth century. His best known book is perhaps The Defeat of the Spanish Armada.

Diplomacy in the modern style, permanent diplomacy, was one of the creations of the Italian Renaissance. It began in the same period that saw the beginnings of the new Italian style of classical scholarship and in the same areas, Tuscany and the valley of the Po. Its earliest flowering came in the same decade in which Masaccio announced a new art of painting on the walls of the Brancacci Chapel and Brunelleschi began the first Italian Renaissance building in the cloister of Santa Croce. Its full triumph coincided with the full triumph of the new humanism and of the new arts, and under the same patrons, Cosimo de'Medici, Francesco Sforza, and Pope Nicholas V. Thereafter, like other creations of the Italian Renaissance, the new diplomacy flourished in Italy for forty years before it was transplanted north of the Alps, and acclimatized in one country after another of Western Europe.

The new diplomacy was the functional expression of a new kind of state. It is simple and easy to say that this new kind of state, 'the state as a work of art', was in turn a primary expression of the creative spirit of the Renaissance. That classic generalization had supplied the foundation for most of what has been written in the last century about Renaissance diplomacy.[1] It does make easy a vivid distinction between the newer style of diplomacy and the older; otherwise it is not very useful. What we see when we look at Italy between 1300 and 1450 is the rise of a number of new institutions and modes of behaviour, among them a new style of diplomacy, all leading to something like a new concept of

---

* From Garrett Mattingly, *Renaissance Diplomacy* (Boston: Houghton Mifflin Company and London: Jonathan Cape Ltd., 1955). Reprinted by permission of the publishers.

[1] Jacob Burkhardt's famous phrase. For an analysis of Burkhardt's influence on historiography see Wallace K. Ferguson, *The Renaissance in Historical Thought* (Cambridge, Mass., 1948).

the state. To label this bundle of ways of acting and thinking and feeling 'the Renaissance State' is unobjectionable. To treat the label as if it were an entity, and say that it was generated by another entity, the spirit of the Renaissance, is explanation only in terms of mythology. It might make better sense to say that the spirit of the Renaissance (whatever that might be) had, among its causes, the evolution of the new state. In this gradual evolution, separate institutional adaptations to changes in the political climate, and consequent acceptance of appropriately changed modes of feeling certainly preceded the finished concept.

The political climate of Italy began to change in the eleventh century. Some of the institutional adaptations, then, are far older than anything we usually call the Renaissance. When the reformed and reforming papacy first defied the German emperors, forces were set in motion which finally burst for Italy the feudal ties in which all the rest of Europe long remained entangled. The energies of the new Lombard and Tuscan communes were set free. By the aid of those energies the papacy tamed the violence of Barbarossa and survived its mortal struggle with Frederick II. By their aid the popes triumphed, and the Guelph party shattered with revolutionary violence the last props of German feudal and imperial dominance. Except for the overshadowing papal and Angevin power, the burghers of Lombardy and Tuscany were left masters of their own political future. By the early fourteenth century, the decline of the Neapolitan kingdom and the failure and humiliation of the papacy cleared the board.

After the popes withdrew to Avignon, Italy was a political vacuum, a gap in the medieval system of hierarchically ordered duties and loyalties. The vacuum had to be filled by the political inventiveness of Italians. After the Emperor Charles IV's subsidized excursion to Rome to collect the imperial crown like a tourist's souvenir, the party warcries of Guelph and Ghibelline lost meaning. When, in another twenty years, the legates of Avignon re-established the temporal sway of the papacy in central Italy, it was the great Guelph republic Florence which, with eloquence and gold, with hired arms and the new weapons of diplomacy, fought the papal forces to a standstill. The temporal authority of the popes could only be readmitted to Italy if it accepted equality with those purely temporal powers which had grown up under its shadow.[2]

[2] A. Gherardi, 'La guerra degli Otto Santi' in *Archivo Storico Italiano*, Ser. 3, vol. V (1867), pt. ii, 35, 131 for the war of the Florentines against Gregory XI. Nino Valeri, *Signorie e principati*, 1343–1516 (Verona, 1949), provides the best general guide to the history of Italy during the whole period. Good critical bibliography.

It was one of the paradoxes of the papal revolt against the emperor that it produced the first and for a long time the only, purely secular states in Christendom. Everywhere else temporal powers were masked and sanctified by religious forms, by priestly consecrations and unctions with holy oil, just as they were at once buttressed and confined by fundamental laws and ancient constitutions, and elevated and immobilized by their position as keystones in the intricately interlocking arches of European feudalism. But in Italy, power was temporal in the strictest sense of the term. It was naked and free, without even the most tenuous connexion with eternity. Fundamentally it was illegitimate, the unanticipated by-blow of a clerical revolt and thus an anomaly in the ordered hierarchy of divinely legitimated rights. Its theorists might dream of republican and imperial Rome. Its custodians might occasionally buy themselves an imperial or a papal title to turn an immediate profit. But they knew that the key to power was force. Thus, in Italy the struggle between the two heads of Christendom cleared the ground for the planting of the first omnicompetent, amoral, sovereign states.

The pragmatic and provisional nature of power made all temporal authority quite literally temporary authority. It depended on the ability of the rulers to compel by force an unhabitual obedience, and on the voluntary allegiance of enough citizens to permit the use of force against the rest. The insecurity of their tenure made the rulers, whether tyrants or oligarchs or dominant factions of the burgher class, alert, uneasy, self-conscious. They had to be sensitive to every threat from within or without. Just 'to maintain the state', just, that is, to keep the current government from being overthrown, was a grave, continuous problem. Because the state, in the realistic sense in which Renaissance Italians used the term, that is, the government, the persons or party actually in power, was always beset by enemies. There were implacable exiles, the leaders of the faction out of power, prowling just beyond reach. There were rival cities, eager to make a profit out of a neighbour's difficulties. And there were usually secret enemies conspiring within the gates.

Therefore the state, depending for its survival on power, was compelled constantly to seek more power. It was ruthless to anomalies and inconsistencies which a more stable, traditional authority might have seen with indifference. And it widened its boundaries when it could. Because the state (that is, the government) could not count on the automatic, customary allegiance of its citizens, it had to win and hold that allegiance by intensifying the community's self-consciousness. It had to serve, or appear to serve, at least some of the interests of at least some of its people.

The shortest way to these objectives was by war. War dramatized the state. War focused loyalty by identifying opposition with treasonable comfort to those who were plotting to plunder the city's treasures and bring low her liberties. War, if it injured the trade of a competitor, strengthened a monopoly, or cleared away an obstructive toll, might actually benefit the interests of the merchants who were always worth conciliating, even when they were not themselves in power. And successful war, if it resulted in the conquest of a neighbour, or the wiping out of some enclave within one's boundaries, actually increased the power of a machine which fed on power.

So warfare between city and city became endemic all over northern and central Italy. Only commercial giants like Venice and Genoa could afford to wage their wars on the sea lanes and shake half the peninsula with their quarrels. Mostly the war was with the nearest independent city, a convenient day's journey or so away. Thus Perugia warred with Arezzo, Florence with Siena, Verona with Padua. But whether the distances were more or less, whether the cities were tyrannies or republics great or small, war became the health of the state.

It was also its most dangerous disease. More even than the factional quarrels of the ruling classes and the mounting unrest of the urban proletariat the endemic wars of Italy threatened its communes with the loss of their hard-won liberties. Even the richest and strongest cities found long-continued wars debilitating. And in the end, victory and defeat were almost equally dangerous. If defeat threatened the return of the exiles, victory risked the seizure of power by a successful general.

The chief danger, however, was complete subjugation. Big cities ate smaller ones. The boundaries of the victors widened ominously towards one another. From 1300 on, the number of independent communes dwindled. Florence took Arezzo and then Pisa, Milan absorbed Brescia and Cremona, Venice annexed Verona and Padua. And these victims had been powerful cities, the conquerors of their smaller neighbours before they were conquered in their turn. Unlikely as it seemed that any one of the rivals could succeed in devouring all the others, no city was strong enough to feel really secure. Under jungle law, the price of survival was incessant alertness. One method of providing for this alertness and of countering the dangers of constant war was found in a new style of diplomacy. It was one of the most characteristic adaptations of the Italian cities to their growing pressure upon one another.

These pressures were intensified, just as the internal development of each state was hastened, by the scale of the peninsular environment.

The growth of states of a new kind in Italy was fostered by a favourable ratio between the amount of social energy available and the amount of space to be organized. In any attempt to account for the precocity of Italian Renaissance political institutions, and particularly for their precocity in diplomacy, this point is second in importance only to the peculiarity of the psychological environment of which we have been speaking.

At the beginning of the fifteenth century Western society still lacked the resources to organize stable states on the national scale. On the scale of the Italian city state it could do so. Internally the smaller distances to be overcome brought the problems of transport and communication, and consequently the problems of collecting taxes and maintaining the central authority, within the range of practical solution. The capital wealth and *per capita* productivity of the Italian towns may not have been very much greater (it was certainly somewhat greater) than that of the more prosperous regions north of the Alps. But the relative concentration of population and the restricted area to be administered enabled the Italian city states to find the means necessary for the ends of government to an extent long impossible to the sprawling, loose-jointed northern monarchies. In consequence, not only was the natural pull of each capital intensified by the regular activities of paid officials, but the whole state was able to mobilize its forces with rapidity and ease rarely possible beyond the Alps.

In external relations, scale had a double effect. The comparative efficiency of the new Italian states (in part a function of their limited areas) enabled them to pursue the objectives of their foreign policy with greater continuity and agility than Europe could show elsewhere. At the same time, the presence within the limited space of upper Italy of armed neighbours, equally efficient, agile and predatory, made continuous vigilance in foreign affairs a prime necessity.

North of the Alps the greater spaces to be overcome made the clash of foreign policies less continuous and less menacing. A Philippe le Bel, an Edward III, a Henry V might be just as aggressive, ambitious, and unscrupulous as any Italian tyrant, and such a king might be capable of summoning from his realm a spurt of energy comparable in intensity to the best Italian effort and, of course, enormously more formidable in size. But such bursts of energy proved sporadic. Because they had not yet succeeded in organizing their own internal space, the feudal monarchies were incapable of really sustained exertions, and the more they were driven towards it, the more likely they were to sink back into regional indifference and factional strife. Meanwhile, the relatively vast

and unorganized spaces of transalpine Europe cushioned political conflicts.

'Vast spaces' is scarcely an exaggeration. We are accustomed to thinking of space as having shrunk in our day. We are vaguely aware that
Moscow is nearer to Chicago now than London was to Paris in Napoleon's time. But we are not so aware that space has been shrinking,
though at a slower rate, for a good many centuries, and that in terms of
commercial intercourse, or military logistics, or even of diplomatic
communication, European distances were perceptibly greater in the
fourteenth century than in the sixteenth, and remained greater in the
sixteenth than they were to become by the eighteenth.[3] In the fourteenth
and fifteenth centuries, the continental space of Western Europe still
impeded any degree of political organization efficient enough to create
a system of continuous diplomatic pressures. Rulers might indulge
themselves in foreign adventures out of vainglory or greed or spite; they
were not yet compelled to continuous vigilance and continuing action
beyond their own frontiers by constant, unavoidable pressures.

It was otherwise in Italy. In upper Italy, by about 1400, space was
becoming completely organized; political interstices were filling up;
the margins and cushions were shrinking, and the states of the peninsula were being obliged by the resulting pressures to a continuous
awareness of each other. Italy was beginning to become such a system
of mutually balanced parts in unstable equilibrium as all Europe was
to be three hundred years later, a small-scale model for experiments with
the institutions of the new state.

For this model to work freely, one other condition was necessary:
a relative isolation. For more than a century, from about 1378 to 1492,
Italy did enjoy that condition. The schism of the papacy, the impo-

---

[3] There is no even partially adequate study of the logistic factor in European
history before the sixteenth century. Some idea of courier speeds *cir.* 1500 may
be gathered from Pierre Sardella, *Nouvelles et speculations à Venise au début du
XVIᵉ siècle* (Paris, n.d. 1947?), and of their progressive decrease in H. Robinson,
The British Post Office (Princeton, 1948) and E. Vaillé, *Histoire générale des
postes françaises* (Paris, 1947, 1949). Both Robinson and Vaillé tend, however,
to distort the problem by following the general custom of citing minimum times,
records for the period over the course. Such records are of far less importance for
the political and economic history of Europe than the normal speeds, and the
volume and regularity of the traffic. Sardella's statistical approach to this question
would seem to be capable of wide and fruitful application. For the consequences
of the logistic factor from the tenth to the thirteenth centuries, see Marc Bloch,
La société féodale: La formation des liens de dépendance (Paris, 1949), pp.
99–115; and for some suggestive remarks on the 'greater size' of the Mediterranean
world in the sixteenth century, Fernand Braudel, *La Méditerranée et le monde
méditerranéen à l'époque de Philippe II* (Paris, 1949), pp. 309–24.

tence of the Empire, the long misery of the Hundred Years War, the recurrent anarchy of the Iberian realms, produced all round Italy a series of crises and conflicts which diverted European pressures from the peninsula. Not that Italy was ever long free from the intrusion of some foreign adventurer in quest of a crown, a lordship or a subsidy. Not that there was ever a decade in which some Italian power was not intriguing to call in a foreigner in order to gain for itself some local advantage. But the foreign intrusions were all on what one may call an Italian scale. None of them threatened more than briefly to become unmanageable, or to alter radically the peninsular balance.

The final result of this long immunity from serious foreign threats was to make Italian statesmen insensitive to the difference in scale between their system and that of Europe, blind to the fact that the tallest giants among the Italian states were pigmies beside the monarchies beyond the Alps. They grew rashly confident of their ability to summon the barbarians when they might be useful and send them home if they became embarrassing. Thus, in the end they failed to understand the catastrophe that overwhelmed them. But the immediate result of the absence of severe outside pressures was to set the states of Italy free for their competitive struggle with one another, and so to intensify their awareness of the structure and tensions of their own peninsular system.

Mainly it was these tensions that produced the new style of diplomacy. Primarily it developed as one functional adaptation of the new type of self-conscious, uninhibited, power-seeking competitive organism. But relatively secondary factors had some influence: the character of Italian warfare and the trend of upper class Italian culture.

Warfare in Italy had changed as busy, pecuniary-minded citizens turned over more and more of the actual fighting to professional soldiers. These were recruited from the more backward regions of the peninsula and commanded by generals who were, in effect, large-scale contractors. Wars waged by mercenary troops under generals mainly zealous for their own professional reputation tended to be less bloody and less decisive than the earlier clashes of citizen militias, though still painfully expensive. War became more rational and, therefore, if less glorious, more civilized.[4] But for this very reason, as campaigns became more and more a series of manoeuvres for political advantage, conducted by relatively small bodies of not always trustworthy professionals, the

[4] Piero Pieri, *La crisi militare italiana nel Rinascimento nelle sue relazioni con la crisi politica ed economica* (Naples, 1934). W. Block, *Die Condottieri* (Berlin, 1913); E. Ricotti, *Storia delle compagnie di ventura* (Turin, 2nd ed., 1893).

management of wars made increasing demands upon statesmanship. Success now depended less upon the brutal shock of massed force than upon vigilant and agile politics. The diplomat was needed to supplement the soldier.

At the same time the dominant elements in Italian society began to set a higher value on a form of contest in which their leading citizens, not mercenary strangers who might change sides for the next campaign, were the champions. Businessmen were delighted by the skills of the diplomat, the nimble anticipation of the next move on the chess board, the subtle gambit which could trip a stronger opponent, the conversion of an enemy into a partner against some common rival, the snatching of victory from defeat by bluff and persuasion and mental dexterity. These qualities were surely more admirable than the brute valour of the condottiere. Diplomacy was for rulers; war for hired men.

It was also natural for the ruling groups—merchants and professional men—most of them with some legal or notarial training (the practical basis of a humanistic education) and most of them experienced in the haggling of the forum and the market place—to believe that words might be as potent as swords. The faith of the merchants and the politicos in the efficacy of diplomatic and forensic persuasion as an auxiliary to or substitute for military force was probably heightened by the reviving interest in classical literature. In turn, no doubt, this faith strengthened the new humanism and helped to give it its prevailing bias towards public rhetoric. The real effectiveness of this form of psychological warfare no one can hope to estimate now. Certainly public opinion among the educated classes was more or less susceptible to propaganda, and certainly, from the time of Petrarch and Cola de Rienzi onward, there was an increasing tendency to try to manipulate this opinion by literary means.[5]

One may be permitted to doubt that an oration by Coluccio Salutati really fell into the scales of political decision with the weight of a thousand horse, but the straight-faced ascription of such a remark to Salutati's most formidable antagonist reminds us of the norm of Renaissance judgement. In that judgement the importance to the state of the diplomat's power of public persuasion, of his ability to deliver a moving formal speech or compose an effectively argued state paper, was at least equal to his utility as an observer, reporter and manipulator of events. In both his aspects, as public orator and as secret negotiator, the fifteenth-century Italian tended to value the successful diplomat with

[5] E. Santi, *Firenze e i suoi 'oratori' nel quattrocento;* C. Curcio, *La politica italiana del' 400* (Florence, 1932).

or above the successful general. Not because 'the business of an ambassador is peace', but because the diplomat, like the general, was an
agent for the preservation and aggrandizement of the state.

EUROPEAN EQUILIBRIUM IN THE
SEVENTEENTH CENTURY *

G. N. Clark

*Sir George Clark is Fellow of All Souls College, Oxford, an authority
on the seventeenth century, and the principal editor of the* New Cambridge Modern History.

For the time being, and indeed for a long time still ahead, international relations could be organized only in such ways as the existence of
jealous separate sovereignties permitted. Under that limitation some
progress was made. The body of the rules of international law grew
in bulk and was much improved in such qualities as adaptability to
the varied circumstances which resulted from the rich experience of
that century of expanding intercourse. A large number of treaties were
concluded by which two or more powers agreed to observe certain rules
between themselves. Often, indeed, there were differences between the
rules accepted in this way by one set of powers and those accepted by
others. The disagreements were so great that they gave rise to wars.
The question of the rights of neutral shipping in time of war, for
instance, was one amongst the causes which drove the English into
wars with both the French and the Dutch. And, although in the
settlements of these questions one treaty often followed the lines laid
down by another between other powers, it is impossible to trace any
decided progress towards the general acceptance of any one system of
regulating them. At the end of the century, as at the beginning, the
Dutch stood, on the whole, for the principle of restricting the interference of war with commerce and allowing as much commerce to go
on as was not directly to the advantage of their enemies alone; while the

---

* From G. N. Clark, *The Seventeenth Century* (Oxford: The Clarendon
Press, 1947). Reprinted by permission of the Clarendon Press, Oxford.

English stood for the principle of suppressing and diverting and controlling commerce in every way that could be made harmful to their
enemies and tolerable to the rest of the world. The great controversy
between belligerents and neutrals went through some novel and remarkable phases, but it cannot be alleged that it was any nearer solution at
the treaty of Utrecht than at the time of the Spanish Armada. What
the seventeenth century did for international law as a factor in the life
of states was not so much to make their relations more legal and regular
in their main lines as to give them a great body of experience in the
regular and legal handling of minor questions. In big things, even in
the larger matter of international law, each state was a law to itself,
but in small things each tended more and more to follow a generally
accepted system of forms.

One department in which this tendency was strong was in the
perfecting of the machinery of diplomatic intercourse. Like so many
other institutions, the system of standing diplomacy had its beginnings
in the Middle Ages; but its rise to being a characteristic feature of the
states of Europe belonged to the sixteenth century, and was a necessary
consequence of the growth in that period of the sovereign state for
which foreign policy is a constant function, a matter of necessity,
whether for ambition or for defence or merely for handling the growing
mass of economic and other everyday business. That stage had already
been reached, and in the seventeenth century the network of embassies
and minor missions was continually spreading and thickening. The
circle of states which had to be taken regularly into account in political
calculations was widening for every statesman, and the amount of
current business was in every way increasing. There were, therefore,
more diplomatists, and they were getting more of the specialized training and attitude of a profession. France set the example. The French
administration was in all its departments a model for the rest of Europe,
and in none was its eminence more marked than in this. It reached its
best level in the time of Louis XIV, when French diplomacy had to
undertake tasks of the most exacting difficulty, and was able to solve
them in a series of negotiations which were the envy of its opponents.
The extraordinary intellectual ascendancy of France seemed to be
embodied in her best ambassadors: men like the comte d'Avaux, whose
dispatches became a text-book for the next century,[1] were not merely
talented individuals, but also they had the prestige of a tradition, the
style of a great school. They and the secretaries of state whom they

[1] For the editions see E. Bourgeois and L. André, *Les sources de l'histoire de
France, XVIIe siècle,* vol. ii, no. 1173.

served had devised a thoroughly efficient routine of instructions, reports, dispatches, and memoranda. No other country at that time approached them in the technique of their calling.

This calling, even in France, had not yet completed its progress towards becoming a profession or a 'service', completely differentiated from all others. On important occasions at the end of Louis's reign a mission to him or from him to a foreign prince might still be entrusted to a general, or to an ecclesiastic; other powers lagged behind France in this as in other ways. Earlier in the century negotiators had been in all countries much less a specialized class of persons: to take only well-known names, the president Jeannin was a judge; Rubens and Gerbier were painters. They, however, were employed for extraordinary missions. The resident envoys and ambassadors, who did the daily work of diplomacy, were for the most part men who spent their lives in this work. It was not thought so desirable as employment nearer the person of the prince: it was a kind of honourable exile, not very remunerative, and very willingly exchanged for any moderately dignified ministerial position at home. Most of the men who discharged it belonged, however, to the ruling classes. The more spectacular missions were reserved for noblemen of high rank, and there were noblemen's sons and other persons of quality amongst the regular diplomatists. Philip IV and the archduchess Isabella did not care to employ Rubens because he was a painter, just as Queen Anne, because his birth was low, would not give Mat Prior the highest employments although he was a professional diplomatist as well as a distinguished author. Promotion, as everywhere in those days, went by merit or favour and not by rule: the hierarchy was even more rudimentary than in armies. There was, however, a considerable number of men who were regularly employed in foreign affairs and only in these, either constantly abroad or with spells in the directing department at home.

A number of books were written to lay down the principles of their craft, some of them historical or legal text-books, others attractive collections of advice and reminiscence.[2] They give an idea of the mental equipment which was thought necessary for the career. It was such as could be picked up from observation and reading by a young man who could get himself attached to the person of an ambassador abroad: secretaryships paid by the state were not unknown, but no sovereigns maintained more than a few of them. A knowledge of the Roman civil law was desirable but not essential, and the number of trained civilians

[2] For a readable survey of the latter class see the essay which gives its title to M. Jusserand's *School for Ambassadors*.

who take part in the diplomacy of the different states was not great. Legal questions were commonly referred to the sedentary civilians of the courts. There are scattered instances in the seventeenth century of attempts by governments to institute a regular training for diplomatists. Torcy in 1712 started a course of instruction under M. de St. Parest; but it was not until later in the eighteenth century that this tendency got far. The regius professorships of modern history founded by George I at Oxford and Cambridge are part of it, like the school kept at Strassburg by Schöpflin and Koch. The need for such innovations illustrates the way in which, as we shall notice later, the universities were losing touch with public life. It is significant that, in the time of William III, Lord Halifax, anxious to get a recruit for diplomacy, wrote to the president of Magdalen to ask him not to insist on Joseph Addison's going into orders. 'His arguments were founded upon the general pravity and corruption of men of business, who wanted liberal education.'[3]

A curious symptom of the development of diplomacy towards maturity is the attention paid to questions of etiquette. Formalities still play a greater part in this sphere than perhaps in any other except those of court and ecclesiastical ritual; but in the seventeenth century they reached a fantastic elaboration.[4] They fill a great part of the considerable literature on the rights and duties of ambassadors. The footman's quarrel at Utrecht was immortalized in *The Spectator*,[5] and the street-fight in London in the time of Charles II between the followers of the French and the Spanish ambassadors showed to all the world that precedence was worth bloodshed. The number of such disputes, more or less serious, was infinite. Ministers were constantly occupied with titles, with the forms of address and correspondence, with the right to take the hand of a foreign representative in his own house or elsewhere, with the arrangement of places at table, with all the pedantries of ceremonial. Disputes were more often deliberately ordered than spontaneous: they were useful as methods of delaying business or of picking a quarrel if a quarrel was wanted. It was easy enough to avoid them if dispatch or harmony was preferable; but it is characteristic of the age that they should have been so prevalent even as means to other ends.

[3] Aikin, *Life of Addison*, i. 57–8. A generation earlier Sir Joseph Williamson, after whom Addison was named, had a plan for sending young men abroad at the expense of the Crown to fit them for the public service. Two whom he sent were Dr. William Lancaster and (Bishop) Nicholson, both members of Queen's College, Oxford, of which Williamson had been a fellow.

[4] There is probably a connexion between this and the spread of court formality in general in the sixteenth and early seventeenth centuries from Spain through Italy to the rest of Europe.

[5] No. 481.

One environment was specially favourable and famous for them, that of the congresses. To put it in another way, the use of congresses was a new method of diplomacy, for the working of which, etiquette, amongst other things, had to be altered and adapted. Only one kind of earlier gatherings, the ecclesiastical councils of the later Middle Ages, bore a resemblance, and that by no means a near resemblance, to these congresses. Their origination is one of the great landmarks of the century.[6] In former times the representatives of three or four powers had sometimes met in one place; but it was not until the time came for winding up the Thirty Years' War, which had involved almost all Protestant and Roman Catholic countries, that there was any general European congress. That settlement was effected by the congress of Westphalia, an assembly not merely impressive in comparison with any that had been seen before, but more impressive than any other before the fall of Napoleon. It met while Grotius was still alive. In the two towns of Münster and Osnabrück—in two towns because of the difficulties of precedence which would have arisen if they had met in one—there were gathered together the representatives of every sovereign in Europe except the outlying kings of England, Poland, and Denmark, and the tsar of Russia who was in Europe geographically but scarcely in any other sense. They made the great body of treaties in which the problems of one generation were solved and those of two more set. From that time to our own the diplomatic history of Europe has stridden along from one congress to another. That of Utrecht which closed the era of Louis XIV was reckoned the ninth from this beginning.[7]

In the treaties of Utrecht solemn recognition was given to a principle which was to supply for a long time to come both pretexts for making war and the theoretical basis of treaties of peace, a principle which was, in fact, to be accepted as the ostensible aim of the foreign policy of every important state. This was the principle of the balance of power; . . . it suited the prevalent habits of thought, and . . . closely . . . related to other doctrines current at the time.[8] For the present it must be treated solely in its direct bearing on international relations. So long as it meant that no one power must be allowed to tyrannize over the

[6] For congresses in general and some other points mentioned in this chapter see Satow, *Guide to Diplomatic Practice*, vol. ii, cap. xxv and *passim*.

[7] The Pyrenees 1659; Oliva 1660; Aix-la-Chapelle 1668; Nijmegen 1676–9; Frankfort 1681; Rijswijk 1697; Carlowitz 1699; Utrecht 1712–13.

[8] Sorel, *L'Europe et la révolution française*, i. 33–4. This masterly volume is the best introduction to the diplomatic history of the period. For our immediate subject Dupuy, *Le Principle de l'équilibre et le concert européen* (1909) and Meinberg, *Das Gleichgewichtssystem Wilhelms III und die englische Handelspolitik*, are worth consulting, and among contemporary works D'Avenant's *Essay on the Balance of Power* and *Essay on Universal Monarchy* (1701).

rest, it was a healthy and admirable idea; but unhappily it lent itself to a different interpretation. It has been defined by a great French historian thus: 'Il se forme ainsi entre les grands États une sorte de société en participation: ils entendent conserver ce qu'ils possèdent, gagner en proportion de leurs mises, et interdire à chacun des associés de faire la loi aux autres.' It had a variety of different forms. On one side it was an analysis of the actual constitution of Europe. An early example of it may be quoted from an English writer, which is interesting because it describes not one general equilibrium of Europe, but a number of separate systems. In the *Observations of his Travels* in 1609 ascribed to Sir Thomas Overbury occurs this passage:

'For the relation of this state [France] to others, it is first to be considered that this part of Christendom is balanced between the three Kings of Spain, France and England, as the other part betwixt the Russians, the Kings of Poland, Sweden, and Denmark. For as Germany, which if it were intirely subject to one monarchy, would be terrible to all the rest, so being divided betwixt so many princes, and those of so equal power, it serves only to balance itself, and entertain easy war with the Turk, while the Persian witholds him in a greater. . . . England is not able to subsist against any of the other, hand to hand, but joined with the Low Countries, it can give law to both by sea, and joined with either of them two, it is able to oppress the third as Henry VIII did.'

The idea of a balance of power at sea, distinct from that on land, half expressed in this passage, is to be found in other works of this and the next century.[9] Usually, however, a single general European equilibrium was meant; and this was represented not merely as in fact existing, but as something to be consciously striven after and artificially manipulated by diplomacy. It was not indeed a new invention of statesmanship to attempt this. There are well-known examples of such an endeavour in the sixteenth century—that of Wolsey is the most famous—and David Hume was quite right in pointing out that 'the utmost refinements' of the theory could be traced as early as Demosthenes.[10] What was new in the seventeenth century was the general and official adoption of the formula. Before it found its way into treaties it appeared in the preambles of English acts of parliament. . . . it was foreshadowed by Sully. Fénelon, the typical liberal of the latter part of the century, praised it as the only means of preserving the general peace and welfare. Though he was protesting against the ideas of Louis XIV, it was

[9] Molesworth, *Account of Denmark* (1694), 3rd ed., p. 175; *Bedford Correspondence,* iii. 126.
[10] *Essays,* Part II, no. vii.

not long before the unrepentant French monarchy resorted to it as a justification.

In contrast with other schemes for preserving peace and order, it seemed to have the advantage of facing the facts. It admitted that every state wanted to prevail over its neighbours, and was prone to use its power for ambitious ends. It offered to provide the means by which these ambitions could be made to neutralize each other. Thus it was advocated as a conservative principle. Just as the alliances against Louis XIV were ostensibly meant to restore the settlements of older treaties, so each adjustment of the balance of power was professedly meant to protect the *status quo* against aggression. In practice, however, it was not a static principle, but a method of regulating and facilitating change. The balance of strength, of which the ordinary basis was territorial possession, was restored, when an aggressor was brought to terms, not by restoring the *status quo,* but by a new construction, in which the several great powers had strength in the required proportions, but not in the old quantities or in the old places. The balance was redressed at need by annexations. The states of Europe fell into two classes, on the one hand the great and growing, on the other those which were declining and at the expense of which the greater were able to add to their possessions. As each strong state gained, its rivals sought for what were later called 'compensations'. Once partition had started, it was bound to go farther. The public claims of the balance coincided with the separate interests of the states which upheld it; the upholding became profitable to these public-spirited powers themselves, so that one rapacious power could lead the world to a rapacity like its own.

If the states had disinterestedly tried to preserve the equilibrium they would thus, in spite of themselves, have perpetuated the universal scramble for territory. The method of the attempt was the formation of alliances, and it has been observed [11] that all 'systems' or groups of states organized in this way tend to become aggressive. By acquiring power they expose themselves to the temptation to use it without the provocation of an attack from outside. Thus, even the formula by which the diplomacy of the seventeenth century tried to put the best light on its intentions was deceptive. It had in it very little of a rational attempt to manage the world's affairs for the general advantage. The smoothness of its professions and the expert plausibility of its apologists easily lead a modern reader to overrate the real quality of its statesmanship. In reality it was penetrated by the spirit of what the French call 'une politique d'aventure'. Only in the countries which were governed

[11] Bernard, *Four Lectures on Diplomacy* (1868) p. 70.

by assemblies was it in any serious sense responsible to public opinion, and, even in those, foreign affairs, except when they touched economic interests, were often and easily kept in the hands of ministers and courtiers. Callières, who had been one of the French plenipotentiaries at Rijswijk, wrote a sentence which was to remain true long after his time: 'La plupart des grandes affaires ont été conclus par des Ministres envoyez secrètement.' [12] It had been so in the treaties of Westphalia, of the Pyrenees, of Rijswijk: it was to be so at Utrecht. The great congresses were something more than a mere façade, but they were not all they seemed to be.

This defect in the conduct of international relations was not accidental. It was intimately related to the whole state of civilization at the time. A sounder and more enlightened diplomacy could not have been produced while the state of politics and especially of political knowledge remained as it was. Alliances and wars were necessarily speculative. The absence of statistical information which we have already noticed as one of the governing conditions of economic life extended, needless to say, also over the political sphere. In the middle of the eighteenth century Lord Chesterfield, as good an authority on this point as could be wanted, wrote to his son: 'There is one part of political knowledge which is only to be had by inquiry and conversation: that is, the present state of every power in Europe with regard to the three important points of strength, revenue and commerce.' [13] In the rest of their correspondence there are abundant proofs of it; but by Chesterfield's time the stock of information available for the public and the machinery by which more could be procured for ministers had far outdistanced what it had been even at the end of the previous century. Huge misconceptions of the strength of an ally, the weakness of an enemy, the obstacles to a campaign or the value of a conquest were almost inevitable in the days of Charles XII and Peter the Great, as in those of Philip II and Queen Elizabeth. Such uncertainty encouraged the spirit of speculation, which on its good side meant adventure and enterprise, on its bad the abandonment of honesty and responsibility. There were far-sighted statesmen here and there; but they had to work with a clumsy, erratic, and dangerous machinery.

[12] *De la manière de négocier* (1716), p. 239.
[13] 1/2 March 1748, no. lviii in Bradshaw's edition.

DIPLOMACY IN THE EIGHTEENTH CENTURY *

Richard N. Rosecrance

Richard N. Rosecrance is Associate Professor of Political Science at the University of California, Los Angeles, and a student of military affairs. He is editor of The Dispersion of Nuclear Weapons.

I

The conditions of international relations under the *ancien régime* were far different from those of the present. Indeed, those of us reared in the twentieth century may find it difficult even to comprehend the international situation prior to the French Revolution. The term, "international," scarcely applies to the relations among states during the eighteenth century. "Nations" had yet to be invented; diplomacy referred to the relations between states governed by aristocrats and monarchs, not to the connections of nations or peoples. The absence of modern nationalism and fervent patriotism sanctioned and supported an interstate polity which was moderate by today's standards. Because the individual inhabitant did not identify himself *primarily* with government or nation, the government could not require or expect his unlimited obedience. In an era in which the channels of communications between people and government were limited or indirect, individuals could not regard the acts of the ruling elite as their own acts.

Modern nationalism could not arise in Europe until communication among members of a society had reached a high peak of intensity. In France, nationalism awaited popular establishment of direct channels of influence or control over government; by constituting for themselves a common government to act in their behalf, the French were welded into a national unit, and in so doing the process of nation-building which had been the work of centuries was completed. Popular

government, or popular influence upon government, then, was the
agency of a heightened communication among Frenchmen which fostered nationalism.[1] In Europe, nationalism was brought not by the
principle of popular sovereignty, but as a result of the new patterns of
communications ensuing from the French incursion in Europe. Nationalism in France was generated on behalf of the revolution, nationalism
in Europe against it, but in both cases it depended upon the social
upheavals of 1789 and after. It could not attain full stature until the
winds of revolutionary doctrine had buffeted the shaky domestic
structure of the old regime.

The impact of the eighteenth-century conservative domestic order
upon diplomacy was far-reaching. Because the French Revolution had
not happened to generate full-blown nationalism, the international
policy and wars of the old regime were largely the business of aristocracies and monarchs.[2] The individual subject usually managed to avoid
involvement, and he was frequently able to pursue his private enterprises wherever they took him in time of war or peace. If these projects
required traveling in an enemy country and fraternizing with its
citizenry, there was no disadvantage. As the war in question was fundamentally the personal affair of Louis XV or Prince Kaunitz, the man in
the street was not himself concerned. Laurence Sterne, English writer
and cleric, was pleased to visit France during the Seven Years' War
between France and his country, to associate with French literati, and
when he returned to England, to praise French life and manners before
his English associates. There was no need to bear malice toward the
French king; his enemy was not England but George III and Mr. Pitt.

Not only was nationalist patriotism impossible in this moderate age,
a kind of European cosmopolitanism further limited parochial sentiment.[3] The subjects of the ruling princes traveled freely in Europe,

[1] R. R. Palmer, "Frederick the Great, Guibert, Bulow: From Dynastic to
National War" in Edward Mead Earle (ed.) *Makers of Modern Strategy* (Princeton, 1953), p. 50. It is worth remarking that popular influence upon government
had proceeded farthest in England and that England was consequently the most
national state prior to the French Revolution.

[2] Professor Leo Gershoy in *From Despotism to Revolution, 1763–1789* (New
York, 1944) argues that the limitations upon wars and the pursuit of power were
purely technical. See pp. 162–165.

[3] See *ibid.*, p. 235. Professor Dorn writes: "In spite of their babel of tongues,
their bloody and endless quarrels, Europe still remained a vital and organic
unity. The wrongs and injuries which these peoples had done one another in
the past, their conquests and reconquests, groupings and regroupings, their occasional fierce hatreds arising from balked ambitions, had welded them into a kind
of union from which even Englishmen, in spite of their insularity, have been
unable to escape to this day." *Competition for Empire, 1740–1763* (New York,
1940), pp. 2–3.

savoring the customs of other countries and comparing them with those of their own.[4] The result of this continual intermingling of Europeans was the gradual development of a hospitality to variant ideas and institutions which transcended geographical frontiers. The age of the Enlightenment strengthened this European cosmopolitanism among the leaders of opinion.[5] The *philosophes* spoke not of men, but of man, and they assumed rational faculties had no relation to political boundaries. If certain social arrangements were archaic in one country, they might be unsuitable in others; if certain laws had utility in one state they might be commended to others.[6] In this unique age, the European was apt to find more in common with members of his own class in another country than with members of a different class in his own. Indeed, it may well be true that in several countries of Europe during the eighteenth century, the social classes were more international in their interests and outlook than they have been at any time since the French Revolution. Marxian "internationalism" may have been more applicable in 1760 than in 1890.[7]

The cosmopolitanism and moderation of this pre-nationalist age found expression in many ways. It decreed that the national origin of monarch, prince or aristocrat should not be of fundamental importance for the social cohesion of a state. As Professor Mowat says, "Peoples accepted rulers from other countries with equanimity." [8] The catalogue of foreign rulers of the *ancient régime* is impressive. A prince of Hanover became King of England; a Duke of Lorraine was made Grand Duke of Tuscany and this same Grand Duke later became Emperor of Germany; the Spanish monarch was a Bourbon grandson of Louis XIV; and the greatest of Russian royalty after Peter the Great was initially a Princess of Anhalt. If peoples were content to put up with rulers of various nationalities, rulers were no less tolerant. They were happy to have subjects of varying national colorations as long as they added to the stock of state power and glory. It is perhaps worth mentioning that Austria was quite willing to take the Spanish Netherlands

---

[4] R. B. Mowat, *The Age of Reason* (Boston, 1934), p. 24.

[5] A brilliant and compact summary of the age of the Enlightenment occurs in Dorn, *op. cit.*, Chapter Five. Professor R. R. Palmer's *The Age of the Democratic Revolution: A Political History of Europe and America, 1760–1800* (Princeton, 1959) illustrates clearly the internationalization of reformist notions during the eighteenth century.

[6] Montesquieu, who pointed out the influence of climate on political organization, would constitute an exception to this generalization.

[7] It did not follow from this that European social classes were homogeneous. See Gershoy, *op. cit.*, Chapter Two.

[8] Mowat, *op. cit.*, p. 23.

as recompense for her endeavors in the War of Spanish Succession despite the fact that the new territories were not Austrian ethnically, and were not contiguous to any Austrian possession.

The internationalism of peoples and rulers infected militarism as well. If the European princes were eager to acquire heterogeneous territories, they were equally disposed to employ recruits from other states in their armies.[9] "All the Continental armies of the eighteenth century contained numerous foreigners, whole regiments of them." [10] Foreign units of the French army were composed typically of Swiss Guards, and Irish units were also used when the French could recruit them. Scottish regiments were regularly found in the service of Holland. The French army before the Revolution was half-composed of men who were not French; and the army of Frederick William I was one-third foreign. Frederick the Great's army some years later was more than half-filled with foreign mercenaries, prisoners of war and deserters from enemy armies.[11] But this was not the extent of the internationalization of warfare. The Prince de Ligne tells the story of a single warrior who was simultaneously or successively a colonel of a regiment of French infantry and of a regiment of German cavalry, chief of a Spanish expedition, captain of a Spanish ocean-going vessel, and a major general in the Spanish army. He was an "officer-general in the service of three countries whose languages he did not know, and the most brilliant vice-admiral Russia has ever had." [12] This man was recognized in Madrid as a nobleman of Spain and in the German states as a Prince of the German Empire. This outstanding example of the cosmopolitanism of the officer class was roughly paralleled by the internationalization of the common soldiery. As one writer noted, "The common soldier was a sort of workman of the military corporation, who toured the world and stopped wherever the trade was good—that is, where war, falling upon some fat country, could nourish its artisan." [13]

But eighteenth-century militarism was not only affected by the prevailing internationalism of the age, it was also moderated by other factors. As a result of the intellectual onslaughts of the philosophers, the chivalrous virtues of courage and honor were at a nadir, and the new virtues of national loyalty and patriotism had not yet taken their

[9] Dorn, op. cit., pp. 98–99.

[10] Mowat, op. cit., p. 51. See also Theodore Ropp, War in the Modern World (Durham, N.C., 1960), pp. 36–37.

[11] It should be noted that during the Seven Years' War the proportion of native troops rose to two-thirds of the whole. See Dorn, op. cit., p. 94.

[12] Prince de Ligne, Memoires, quoted in Mowat, op. cit., p. 54.

[13] E. Lavisse, La Jeunesse du Grand Frederic, quoted in ibid., p. 55,

places. In the interim, the career of the soldier was scarcely a glamorous one. Even in France, which maintained the most truly national army prior to the revolution, cafés and other public places displayed signs reading: "No dogs, lackeys, prostitutes or soldiers." [14] But the inhospitable climate of opinion was not the only handicap to a fully developed militarism. Because of the exemption of the nobility from taxation, governmental revenues were limited; deficient resources meant that the professional mercenary armies employed by the monarch would be expensive. "Each soldier represented a heavy investment in time and money. Trained troops lost in action could not easily be replaced." [15] Thus, armies were valuable mechanisms which could not be hazarded in chance engagements. In this context, the threatened destruction of a prince's army was a potent reason for immediate peace, and armies were as prized as provinces.

The military machine of the old regime was additionally hindered in that certain classes of value to the state were freed from military service. Classes deemed productive, the bourgeoisie and higher peasantry were not expected to find places in the army.[16] As one writer has phrased it, the militarism of the old regime ". . . was built on an economy that did not tolerate the removal of its useful members for military purposes. The big armies were thus composed of economically exempt classes. . . ." [17]

As a result of the inadequate rewards of status and prestige attendant on military service, the professional soldier had to be well-paid and well-nourished, or he would desert. The consequence was a dependence upon long baggage trains and an elaborate system of supply magazines, both of which imposed severe limits on military mobility. Armies had to be marched in formation to be held together; forced marches, campaigns in the forest, and night marches provided irresistible opportunities for desertion.[18] It is not surprising that Frederick the Great believed that his armies could be maintained intact only if his soldiers feared Prussian officers more than the enemy.

The limitations upon the composition and maintenance of armies affected the strategy which might be employed. Because armed forces were expensive and delicate mechanisms, large-scale pitched battles between whole armies were studiously avoided. Battles could not be

[14] Palmer, *loc. cit.*, p. 50.
[15] *Ibid.*, p. 51
[16] See Dorn, *op. cit.*, p. 81.
[17] Hans Speier, "Militarism in the Eighteenth Century," *Social Research*, Vol. 3, No. 3 (1936), p. 336.
[18] See Dorn, *op. cit.*, p. 82.

fought until a battle line had been drawn and formations arranged; dispersed field attacks were rejected as presenting too strong a temptation to desertion. Battle of any sort was a considerable risk, and victory, if it entailed the decimation of the victorious force, was not to be sought. It was natural that military thinkers believed that a state might lose as much from victory as from defeat. Even when a battle gave the edge to one force, it might not be able to pursue its advantage; armies might be defeated in the confrontation of the battlefield, but it was more difficult to destroy them in full retreat. Battles, in any case, did not end wars, because they were seldom decisive. As Professor Palmer notes: ". . . the contrast between eighteenth-century and Napoleonic battles is especially clear. After Blenheim, Malplaquet, Fontenoy or Rossbach, the war dragged on for years. After Marengo, Austerlitz, Jena, Wagram or Leipzig, peace overtures began in a few months." [19] A strategy of annihilation could not be followed until after the French Revolution; the old regime had to be satisfied to wage wars of maneuver and position. The anachronistic social system of the *ancien régime* prevented the utilization of military resources which otherwise might have been tapped; wars, therefore, were limited both in terms of the standards of the age and those of a more modern era.

The prevailing moderation and internationalism of the period applied to diplomacy as well as warfare. As there was an international soldiery, there was also an international corps of diplomats and statesmen to serve Europe's crowned heads. "Nobody was excluded from employment, even from the highest official positions, on account of nationality." [20] It is often not recognized that one of the pre-eminent characteristics of "French-style" diplomacy was its European character. [21] Some European courts selected their statesmen and diplomats from certain favored foreign nations. The Danes had a penchant for Germans at the helm of state, and for twenty years a Hanoverian was the center of a Danish ruling clique. So great was his ascendancy that Frederick the Great was reputed to have coined the epigram: "Denmark has her fleet and her Bernstorff." [22] When the latter finally fell in 1770, he was succeeded by another German, a Dr. Struensee who, though he was the virtual ruler of Denmark for two years, never learned Danish.

[19] Palmer, *loc. cit.*, p. 52.

[20] Mowat, *op. cit.*, p. 16.

[21] See Harold Nicolson, *The Evolution of Diplomatic Method* (London, 1954), Chapter Three.

[22] W. F. Reddaway, "Denmark under the Bernstorffs and Struensee," in A. W. Ward, G. W. Prothero, and Stanley Leathes (eds.) *The Cambridge Modern History,* Vol. 6, The Eighteenth Century (New York, 1909), p. 740.

The Russians, governed by a foreign empress, sought statesmen from two foreign nationalities. The English provided their naval leadership and the Germans were found at the court. John Elphinston and Sir Samuel Greig were given high positions in the Russian Admiralty and one Peter Lacy became a Russian general. For her immediate entourage, Catherine II chose a German named Biren as her Grand Chamberlain.

The Spanish, however, surpassed all others in their appropriation of foreign talent. They were absolutely promiscuous in their choice of foreign public servants. Elizabeth Farnese brought Alberoni from Parma to become diplomatic dictator of Spain. Later another Italian, the Marquis of Squillaci, was made Minister of War and Finance. But Italians were not the only group to become entangled in the sinuosities of the Spanish court. Baron Ripperda, a Dutchman, played a brief but important role in Spanish diplomacy. He was born a Catholic in Groningen, but embraced Protestantism to qualify for the Dutch public service. When he deserted Holland to serve the Spanish monarch, first as an emissary of Alberoni and later as chief minister, he reverted to Catholicism. After his disgrace in 1726 he fled to Morocco, became a Mohammedan, and fought in a war against Spain. When Ripperda fell, his influence with Elizabeth was bequeathed to an Austrian, Konigsegg, the Habsburg ambassador. And the limits of Spanish tolerance had not yet been approached; Austrians, Italians, and Dutchmen were ably abetted by Irishmen at the Spanish court. Richard Wall was Spanish foreign minister for several years; Alexander O'Reilly was a Spanish general and Minister of War; and Sir Thomas Fitzgerald became Spanish Ambassador in London. England and France, in some ways the most conservative in their national outlooks, were not exempt from a proclivity for foreigners. George I surrounded himself with influential Hanoverians, and France gave positions of great importance to the Scotsman, John Law, and the Genevese, Jacques Necker.

The internationalization of statecraft had significant consequences. If the compulsions of nationalism could not be invoked to ensure faithful service, diplomats and intriguers could only be appeased by a liberal distribution of state funds. Between 1757 and 1769 the French subsidized Austrian officials to the extent of 82,652,479 livres, and Kaunitz himself was ransomed to the extent of 100,000 livres. The French Abbé (later Cardinal) Dubois offered the English minister Stanhope 600,000 livres for a treaty of alliance with France. (The offer was gracefully declined, but Dubois was invited to Stanhope's house for informal conversations, and in due course a treaty was signed.) The practice of "diplomatic compensation" continued until well after the French Revolution. A Prussian diplomat in Paris summarized the situation well when he wrote in 1802: "Experience has taught everybody who is here on diplomatic business that one ought never to give anything before the deal is definitely closed, but it has also proved that the allurement of gain will often work wonders." [23] It was not only commonplace to bribe foreign emissaries, it was necessary to reward foreigners who agreed to spy or to carry on secret missions for European sovereigns. During the eighteenth century the French paid to potential spies and intriguers huge sums, generally to no practical end. In some cases systematic corruption usurped the role of traditional diplomacy. Between 1764 and 1771 Denmark, Russia, and England on the one side, and France on the other, waged an overt war of bribery for the soul and allegiance of Sweden. The first three, spending fantastic sums, seemed to have won victory when the death of Adolphus Frederick unexpectedly gave the French the upper hand.

Despite the venality of the age, money could not gain every desired goal. There were some things which the European monarchs would not stoop to do even though great issues hung in the balance. During the Seven Years' War a French agent in England proposed the destruction of the Bank of England by counterfeiting British pounds and presenting them at the Bank for payment in specie. Louis XV, however, rejected the project as ungentlemanly and claimed that it aroused his indignation and horror. When, thirty years later, the Austrian Emperor was given a similar opportunity, he gave a like reply. At another time a young Russian nobleman offered to betray his own father in order to give English state secrets to the French, but Louis and his advisers demurred. "It is, in general," the French King wrote, "too dangerous to trust a man who betrays his most sacred duties." [24]

II

The conditions of social organization, diplomacy, militarism, and statesmanship in the eighteenth century led to the creation of a system of international relations which was unique in the history of statecraft and unlike any system functioning today. These conditions fulfilled

[23] Quoted in Hans J. Morgenthau, *Politics among Nations* (New York, 1956), p. 222.

[24] Quoted in J. W. Thompson and S. K. Padover, *Secret Diplomacy: A Record of Espionage and Double-Dealing: 1500–1815* (London, 1937), p. 162. It should of course be remarked that subornation was not limited to the old regime. Corruption and bribery continued during the nineteenth and twentieth centuries though they were no longer a major *modus operandi* of the international system.

almost completely the ideal precepts for a balance of power mechanism. A balance of power apparatus could not function without the existence of a state system, "that is, a group of independent 'neighboring states more or less connected with one another' and of relatively equal power"; [25] it could not operate without a minimal homogeneity of political attitude among the participating state units and a common concern to protect the system; it could not maintain itself without a limitation of warfare to preserve the constitutent state-components. The eighteenth century met the requirements for a balance of power mechanism in all these ways, and the maxims of balance of power theory were obeyed as never before or since.

Because of the lack of popular government, the subjects of prince or aristocracy did not identify themselves with the acts of their ruling cliques—in short, the absence of popular government decreed an absence of nationalism. King or lord could not assume popular approval for his diplomacy or wars; hence, he could carry neither to extremes; none of Europe's crowned heads could expect subject populations to make great sacrifices at the altar of *raison d'état*. The consequence of the limited diplomacy which resulted from this condition can scarcely be overestimated. It was, fundamentally, that the eighteenth century was destined to be a moderate, or as some have called it, an "admirable" age in international relations.[26]

But "limited diplomacy" was not the only result of the social and political system of the old regime. The limited revenues of the eighteenth-century states, the exemption of economically productive classes from military service, the systematic denigration of military virtues, and the internationalism of the professional soldiery combined to produce an erudite warfare of siege and maneuver. In practice this entailed wars of limited objectives and the drawing of a viable distinction between soldier and civilian. The military machine of the old regime was ideally suited to the maintenance of the state system for no great Power could hope to destroy others with the limited resources and uncertain loyalties it commanded. A great Power might be able to protect its own independence and perhaps even advance it, but it could not hope to launch the kind of wholesale onslaught on the European liberties which became commonplace with the French Revolution and the Napoleonic era. As long as limited war held sway, the balance system could not be undermined by a single Power; when the

[25] Edward Vose Gulick, *Europe's Classical Balance of Power* (Ithaca, New York, 1955), p. 4.
[26] See Mowat, *op. cit.*, Chapter One.

"hyperbolic war" of the twentieth century took its place, therefore, the balance machinery was destroyed.

If the archaic social and political systems of the period limited the forms of diplomacy and warfare, they did not circumscribe the range of diplomatic choice available to European royalty. If subjects would not support unlimited *means* in interstate relations, they would not dictate the choice of *ends*. Thus, princes and nobilities enjoyed a wide range of discretion in choosing their avenues of statecraft. If one were to compare the eighteenth century with the present age, the conclusion would be that two hundred years ago political rulers were able to choose their policies in foreign relations within the range of a full circle, but the implementation of policy was severely limited by inadequate popular support. Today, on the other hand, political leaders must select their policies within the range of a short arc, but they may carry out their programs with enormous force and vigor.

But if popular limitations upon the range of policy decision did not exist in the old regime, there were other important limitations. Chief of these was the ethic of the monarch which required that he call his royal peers "brother," and which precluded an unalloyed Machiavellianism. Despite the machinations of the age, the eighteenth century did not approach the amorality of Renaissance intrigue; the interstate relations of the *ancien régime* were manifestations of "French" not "Italian style" diplomacy. As one student has noted, the princes and aristocracies of the eighteenth century, "were joined together by family ties, a common language (French), common cultural values, a common style of life, and common moral convictions about what a gentleman was and was not allowed to do in his relations with other gentleman." [27] The international gentility of the era was well-suited to the preservation and protection of the state system, for it promoted that attention to group interest on which the system rested. A balance of power mechanism could hardly have functioned in a context in which all protagonists were bent on advancing their separate interests against general European concerns.

Nor were these the only elements of eighteenth-century diplomacy which conduced to a self-adjusting balance of power apparatus. A minimum homogeneity of outlook among the great states was prerequisite to such a system, and the necessary unity of sentiment and idea was to be found *par excellence* in the old regime. The eighteenth century, unlike the centuries which preceded and followed it, did not witness great conflicts of principle in the realm of interstate relations.

[27] Morgenthau, *op. cit.*, p. 221. See also Gershoy, *op. cit.*, p. 26.

If it is possible to talk of ideology in this pre-revolutionary age, one could claim with justice that a common ideology of aristocratic and monarchical conservatism, tempered by limited reform, characterized the period. The disastrous religious conflicts of previous centuries no longer disturbed the European peace, and the great social commotions surrounding liberalism, socialism, fascism, and communism had not yet arisen to disturb it once again. The philosophic and programmatic writings of the Enlightenment had not yet generated the conflicts of 1792 and afterward. There were, therefore, no perverse ideological issues to disrupt the free play of a balance mechanism. The balancing system of Europe required states to ally or oppose each other according to the presumed distribution of power: if ideological bonds or animosities had arisen, states could no longer have charted their courses on power considerations alone; states would have refused to balance against their ideological *confrères* or· to align themselves with ideological opponents, regardless of the configuration of power. The absence of divisive intellectual issues then, permitted a European balancing of considerable scope.

The freedom from ideological grievances sanctioned a phenomenal competition for power and empire both within Europe and outside it.[28] The eighteenth century was the age of Franco-British struggles in America, the Caribbean, in Canada and India; it was the time of the enormous Russian territorial expansion at the expense of Sweden, the Ottoman Empire, and Poland; it was the century of Frederick the Great's rape of Silesia and the three partitions of Poland which removed that historical state from the European map, except for a brief interlude, for more than one hundred years. But the pursuit of power and glory was restrained not only by the conservative domestic constitution of Europe's aristocratic states, but also by the balance of power system.[29]

The balance mechanism itself reinforced the internationalism of the century. The equilibrating system presumed the unlimited mobility of each participating state and as the locus of power was constantly in flux, each state would combine alternately with several others. In the process of the *"renversement des alliances"* a state would ultimately sense the presence of a European system of which it was but a single part, and this consciousness would force recognition in turn of the useful role played by other constituent units. In this manner, the perception of a European system led directly to a sentiment of fundamental unity. This minimal consciousness of unity among the European sovereigns

---

[28] Professor Dorn goes so far as to assert: ". . . warfare became a function, if not an actual necessity, of the structure of European society." (*Op. cit.,* p. 5.)

[29] See *ibid.,* pp. 2–3.

was reflected in a tolerance of the Great Powers for one another which permitted each to maintain its basic character. "Intervention" of one Power in another's domestic affairs did not become commonplace until after the French Revolution; nor was it ever an essential principle of eighteenth-century diplomacy.[30] It was, in fact, at odds with the moderate tenor of the age. Intervention only became necessary when some Powers ceased to give serious concern to the maintenance of the system. When France breached the limits of eighteenth-century toleration in overturning the domestic constitutions of conservative states during the Revolutionary and Napoleonic periods, the conservative states, in turn, proclaimed the right of "intervention" to forestall the use of revolutionary force. "Intervention" then, was more nearly a reflection of the breakdown of the balance of power system, than it was an intrinsic principle of it.

In the pre-revolutionary period, Frederick II was perhaps the most Machiavellian of the eighteenth-century monarchs (and, fittingly, the writer of *Anti-Machiavel*); yet, even he did not use the interventionist tactics of Bonapartism. When he launched his unprovoked aggression on Silesia, he did not contemplate the destruction or domestic overturn of the Habsburg monarchy; rather, he sought Silesia as his price for defending the "Pragmatic Sanction" and Maria Theresa. Thus, one should not attempt to read the old regime through Polish glasses. The partitions of Poland were not hallmarks of European relations because Poland was not a constituent member of the European system, and, as Professor Mowat tells us, ". . . Poland was the frontier-country." [31] "Europe" stopped at the Vistula.

The balance of power system of the eighteenth century, however, could not be molded into an effective European Concert. There was no conference of Powers meeting periodically to decide questions of war, peace, and the distribution of power. But this omission revealed the halcyon character of the age: a Concert of Europe could be created only after a period of revolutionary cataclysm and war had spurred men to organize peace and a rudimentary machinery of international government. Though the wars of the *ancien régime* were taxing and violent for those directly involved and often disastrous for the public purse, they were not sufficiently catastrophic to call forth the concerted effort of Europe to prevent their recurrence. Even such a desperate and bloody struggle as the Seven Years' War was mild in comparison to the revolutionary convulsions of a half century later. The absence of a

[30] Cf. Gulick, *op. cit.*, pp. 62–65.
[31] Mowat, *op. cit.*, p. 21.

regular Concert, then, was an indirect tribute to the relative moderation of the century of the old regime.

Despite periods of warfare, the eighteenth century was a generally stable period in international relations. The balance of power mechanism did not prevent military contests, but it did prevent them from getting out of hand. The limited ambitions of European autocrats and cabinets resulted in limited diplomacy and militarism. The outcomes of international politics did not exceed the bounds of convention and precept. There were no permanently dissatisfied major participants in the European state system: a more or less placid stability was the order of the day.

The objectives and techniques of diplomacy were both strictly limited. Prince and monarch had modest ambitions in the international environment, and they had restricted means at their disposal. They did not aim, nor could they expect to overturn the internal constitution of other states. The cosmopolitan internationalism of statecraft and war prevented drastic outcomes in world politics. Europe held itself at bay.

THE CONCERT OF EUROPE *

F. H. Hinsley

F. H. Hinsley, Fellow of St. John's College, Cambridge, and University Lecturer in History at Cambridge, is also the author of Hitler's Strategy.

When the Congress system proved unworkable the notion of a coalition of leading states, founded on a public law for the defence of that law, was not abandoned. It was set free from its earlier association with the determination to govern the world—from the form the Congress idea at first assumed when it at last replaced, at the beginning of the nineteenth century, the aspiration to universal monarchy. A looser association of the Great Powers continued in existence—an attenuated Congress system limited to dealing with problems as they arose, not seeking to anticipate them or to iron them out of existence.

* From F. H. Hinsley, *Power and the Pursuit of Peace* (New York: Cambridge University Press, 1963). Reprinted by permission of the Cambridge University Press.

The public law which was applied to these problems was enriched and reinforced by the passage of time and the growth of precedent but was restricted to what the looser association could agree on, and thus to strictly international questions. These were the two outstanding features of what came to be called the Concert of Europe.

This shift to a looser organisation among the Great Powers was reflected in the terminology of the time. Contemporaries did not define the words Congress and Conference precisely. Because of their inconsistencies it remains impossible to state exactly how they distinguished between the functions of these two forms of international proceeding.[1] But one thing is clear. As Sir Charles Webster noticed, the one consistent difference between a Congress of the Great Powers and a Conference of the Great Powers in the nineteenth century was that a Congress was a meeting attended by the heads of governments or their Foreign Ministers while a Conference was confined (except for the Foreign Minister of the state on whose territory the meeting took place) to the ambassadors accredited to the state where it was held.[2] It is this which gives significance to a further fact which Sir Charles Webster did not sufficiently emphasise. While holding by and large to this distinction, and while taking part in international meetings as frequently as before, the Powers avoided Congresses after 1822. Between 1830 and 1856 there were eight Conferences attended by all the Great Powers; between 1830 and 1884 no less than seventeen. Of Congresses as opposed to Conferences only two were held in the nineteenth century after the Congress of Verona—that of Paris in 1856 and the Congress of Berlin in 1878.[3]

[1] It has been suggested that a Congress was a meeting attended by the smaller states as well as by the Great Powers and that a Conference was a meeting limited to the Great Powers, or that the name Congress was adopted only when a meeting was held to make a peace treaty. Neither of these distinctions can be made compatible with the evidence. A further suggestion [A. J. P. Taylor, *The Struggle for Mastery in Europe* (1954), 83.] is that Conferences were 'limited to specific subjects' whereas a Congress was a 'European' meeting discussing 'the affairs of all Europe'. This ignores two facts: Conferences after 1822 were also 'European' meetings; and the Congresses held up to 1822 were all held to discuss subjects.

[2] Sir Charles Webster, *The Art and Practice of Diplomacy* (1961), 55, 67. The two words were never precisely distinguished even in this way. Thus the Conference of London of 1830-2 was reinforced by special envoys and the British and French Foreign Secretaries were sent out to reinforce the Conference of Vienna of 1855. On the other hand the Congress of Paris was to begin with called a Conference in the official papers. But this difference was clearly one that governments tried to maintain.

[3] Op. cit. 58-9, 69. The following list omits ambassadorial and other conferences which were not conferences of all the Great Powers, and technical meetings on subjects like armaments or the tolls of the Scheldt:

This transition was resisted. Attempts were often made to summon other Congresses; these sometimes reflected the wish to restore the earlier Congress system—the conviction that the system of *ad hoc* Conferences, to which the Powers were being reduced, was inadequate. In 1836 Louis Philippe wanted a Congress to draw up a treaty in accordance with which 'no change, no alienation of territory, would have taken place in future without the concurrence of all the Powers —and I would then have realised the idea I have continually pursued of an *entente* of the five Powers for the solution of all the great political questions . . . , for settling all those questions with a general and European interest . . . , for guaranteeing the *status quo* of the territorial delimitation of Europe.'[4] In 1840 Metternich proposed a league of the other four Powers against France which might be developed into an organisation to maintain the future peace of Europe by the renunciation of force and the establishment of a permanent Conference system.[5] In 1849 Louis Napoleon, the new President of France, suggested a general Congress for the revision of the 1815 treaties.[6] When

Congresses		
Vienna/Paris	1814–15	(Peace Treaty and Quadruple Alliance)
Aix-la-Chapelle	1818	(France)
Troppau	1820	(Revolutions; the Naples Revolution)
Laibach	1821	(Naples Revolution)
Verona	1822	(Italy; Spain; En. Question)
Paris	1856	(Peace Treaty)
Berlin	1878	(En. Question)

Conferences		
London	1830–2	(Belgium)
Rome	1831–2	(Reform of Papal states)
London	1838-9	(Belgium)
Vienna	1839	(En. Question)
London	1840–1	(En. Question)
London	1850–2	(Schleswig-Holstein)
Vienna	1853	(En. Question)
Vienna	1855	(En. Question)
Paris	1858	(Principalities)
Paris	1860–1	(Syria)
London	1864	(Schleswig-Holstein)
London	1867	(Luxembourg)
Paris	1869	(Crete)
London	1871	(Black Sea)
Constantinople	1876–7	(Eastern Question)
Madrid	1880	(Morocco)
Berlin	1884–5	(Africa)

[4] *Ibid.* 57–8, 167–8.
[5] *Ibid.* 176–7.
[6] F. A. Simpson, *Louis Napoleon and the Recovery of France* (3rd edn. 1951), 41–2.

the Powers were negotiating for a meeting in 1859 the Russian Foreign Minister wanted it to be composed of Cabinet Ministers, not of diplomatic agents, and thought it should be called a Congress rather than a Conference, 'as more appropriate to the gravity of the times'.[7] By then such aspirations were beginning to conceal a still more radical discontent. Napoleon III's determination to turn the Conference of 1856 into a Congress, like his proposal of 1863 for a Congress of the European states to revise the Treaty of Vienna,[8] was partly inspired by his dream of remodelling Europe into a federation of free nations in pursuit of his uncle's prophecy that 'the first ruler who calls upon the peoples of Europe will be able to accomplish anything he wishes'.[9] It is perhaps true to say that of all the Great Powers only Great Britain was generally contented with the system which steadily prevailed over these various efforts to go beyond it. Certainly Palmerston was the only statesman in these years to assume Castlereagh's role and oppose these efforts on generalised grounds.

At the first of the nineteenth-century Conferences, in 1830, he was careful to emphasise that 'we, the Conference, have no right to make an arbitrary distribution of Europe upon the principles of the Holy Alliance or the Congress of Vienna.'[10] In 1849, in opposition to Louis Napoleon's wish to hold a Congress to revise the 1815 treaties, he made the same point: France and England were committed to the view that internal questions were not legitimate subjects for the intervention of a Congress; yet it was by such questions, not by international problems, that Europe was being disturbed.[11] Even for international questions he preferred *ad hoc* Conferences to something more formal. In 1841 he

[7] Webster, *op. cit.* 57.

[8] *Ibid.* 57–8, 63.

[9] *The New Cambridge Modern History,* vol. x, 461–2.

[10] Sir Charles Webster, *op. cit.* 65. A further example of his several statements of this opinion was his argument during the Austro-Sardinian war in 1848 that "however dazzling the action . . . of a General Congress of the Great Powers . . . for the purpose of settling all the affairs of Italy and perhaps, also, of other parts of Europe, yet such a scheme would be attended . . . with many practical difficulties, and liable to many objections. . . . The Congress of Vienna . . . was assembled [when] . . . the tide of war had swept over the whole surface of Europe . . . ; all the smaller States . . . had been conquered and reconquered . . . the statesmen who sat in Congress, therefore, considered themselves at liberty to parcel out with great freedom the several territories of Europe. The smaller Sovereigns . . . were all obliged to yield to overruling power. . . . But England, France, Austria, Russia and Prussia have not at present any similar pretence to dispose of the affairs of any of the smaller States . . . , either in Italy or elsewhere. . . .' (Palmerston to Normanby, 10 Oct. 1848. *State Papers,* vol. LI, 672.)

[11] Simpson, *op. cit.* 42.

opposed Metternich's further suggestion that there should be set up at least a permanent Conference to deal with the Ottoman question, and opposed it with the argument that when the agreements reached at the recent conference on Turkey had been implemented 'perhaps the next thing will be that the five Powers and Turkey should fall back into their usual state of reciprocal relations. Concert between Powers and centres of negotiation are useful and necessary when some Treaty is in operation which not only requires, but at the same time regulates, their common action; but it would be difficult to establish a permanent concert unaccompanied by any recorded and specifick engagement.' [12] But it was not only Palmerston who insisted on normally maintaining 'the usual state of reciprocal relations'; and he was right in regarding this as the usual state of diplomacy. The attempts to restore something like the earlier Congress system were mainly frustrated, as they were mainly inspired, by the multifarious rivalries of all the Powers.

It is sometimes said that the revolutions of 1830 divided the Great Powers into two ideological groups, the three autocratic states and the constitutional states of France and Great Britain. This rift had grown up before 1830—Castlereagh had often spoken of it—but it is true that the 1830 revolutions kept it alive. Great Britain immediately recognised Louis Philippe after the French Revolution of 1830 despite Russia's hostility to the new régime and despite the fact that the other four Great Powers could be said to be bound by the Quadruple Alliance to meet together to discuss internal changes in France. Russia, Austria and Prussia publicly recognised in the Münchengratz agreement of 1833 the right of any sovereign to call on them for aid against any revolution; and Palmerston engineered the Quadruple Alliance of 1834 as 'a powerful counterpoint'—to use his own words—'to the Holy Alliance of the East.' [13] In 1835 he publicly identified the interests of England with the constitutional cause in Europe and asserted that the Eastern Powers had a secret treaty to put constitutionalism down.[14] In 1836 he spoke of 'the three and the two, who think differently and therefore act differently'.[15] For another twenty years these sentiments were never far below the surface on both sides, and were always quick to revive—so that Austria and Prussia could sign another treaty against 'the revolution' in 1851,[16] and in 1854 the French ambassador in Constantinople could congratulate Napoleon III on the Austro-French-British

---

[12] Webster, op. cit. 178–9.
[13] Quoted in The New Cambridge Modern History, x, 253.
[14] Sir Charles Webster, op. cit. 165.
[15] The New Cambridge Modern History, x, 246.
[16] A. J. P. Taylor, The Struggle for Mastery in Europe, 43–4.

alliance of that year: 'You have inflicted a mortal blow on the Holy Alliance.'[17] At the same time, however, they were increasingly joined after 1830 by other rivalries which made even settled ideological alignments among the Powers impossible.

On the one hand, with the revival of France, Great Britain found herself cooperating with the Eastern Powers against France as frequently as she cooperated with France against them. This was the pattern during the Belgian crisis of 1831–2, against the French attempt to establish a position of special influence over the new Belgian state. In 1836, though she had been quick to recognise Louis Philippe, she frustrated his plans for a Congress as decisively as did the Russian Government: both suspected that it was not unconnected with the wish to rescue France from the tutelage imposed on her in 1815.[18] On the other hand the growing rivalry of Austria and Prussia in Germany and of Austria and Russia in the Near East produced a similar instability in the eastern camp. Metternich's suggestions of 1840–1 for a permanent conference arose less from concern to restore the old Holy Alliance than from the aim of making Vienna the permanent centre of the European diplomatic system and of enlisting Western aid against Austria's neighbouring Powers. The Tsar opposed them as decisively as did Great Britain, and with words that might have been used by Castlereagh. He told the British ambassador that Metternich must be disabused of his belief that he could 'advise upon every subject' and 'from his closet direct and instruct all the world'.[19] By that date—when France, embittered by commercial and Near Eastern rivalry with Great Britain, was seeking an alliance with Austria; when Great Britain had concluded an agreement with the three eastern Powers against French designs in the Near East; when Russia was asking for still closer relations, for an alliance indeed, with Great Britain as a safeguard against Austria as well as against France—the complex pattern of diplomacy had already been laid down which was to prevail until 1871. It was not simplified by the revolutions of 1848 which revealed that even the autocratic governments would only act, if they would act at all, in their own individual interests. Or by the revival of the Empire in France in 1852—the year in which the British government both welcomed a Russian offer to send 60,000 men to defend Belgian independence if France threatened it and also refused to join the eastern Powers in demanding from Louis Napoleon a guarantee of his peaceful intentions as a condition of

[17] *Ibid.* 70.
[18] Sir Charles Webster, *op. cit.* 168.
[19] *Ibid.* 154–5, 177–9.

recognising the Empire. Or by the first serious result of, among other things, the new Emperor's restless wish to destroy the Vienna settlement and substitute for it a system of weak federal states under the patronage of France—by the Crimean War. The Crimean War only intensified, indeed, those interlocking jealousies and suspicions between all the Great Powers which explain why special factors were needed before they could agree to assemble even in the individual Congress of 1856—they had been at war among themselves—and why the resort to *ad hoc* conferences was as close as they could normally come to collaboration.

Even that looser system was one which proved difficult to operate on account of these rivalries. After the first conference on Belgium Metternich and Palmerston both obstructed the summoning of another to continue its work: each suspected the other of wishing to have it under his control.[20] In 1833 it was impossible to convene a conference on the Eastern Question because each insisted that it should meet in his own capital—that, in Palmerston's words, 'we are on an equal footing . . .'. It was then that Great Britain herself was charged—and by none other than Metternich—with the wish to dominate diplomacy by reviving the Congress system. He accused Palmerston of trying to make the London Conference permanent, 'to raise it to the standing and the influence of an areopagus in which the representatives of the three Continental Powers would be reduced to the role of accomplices in the reformist policies of the two Maritime Courts'.[21] During the next generation, while no conference proved easy to convene and each met only after a fierce struggle concerning its agenda [22] as well as its venue, the assembled Powers were never unanimously contented with the proceedings. Palmerston complained in 1833 that the way in which the Eastern Powers had behaved at the Belgian Conference had made the whole idea of a further Five-Power Conference unpalatable to his Cabinet; [23] but he also noted of the same Conference that 'the three Eastern Courts have been a little jealous of their Plenipotentiaries',[24] and this was an understatement. Their distrust of the proceedings had been so great that they first sought to reduce the Conference's authority and then insisted on its suspension.[25] It was not able to resume until 1839, but then it confirmed the settlement of 1831—delineating

[20] *Ibid.* 158.
[21] *Ibid.* 158–61.
[22] *Ibid.* 62.
[23] *Ibid.* 159.
[24] *Ibid.* 66.
[25] *Ibid.* 67, 157–8.

the boundaries of Holland and Belgium and making Belgium a neutral member of the European states' system under the permanent guarantee of the Great Powers—which had been a self-denying ordinance for all the signatories. The proceedings of another Conference in 1839, that held in Vienna on the Turkish question, were bluntly disowned by the Tsar, and it was his opposition to Vienna as the place for discussion that secured the transfer of the Conference to London.[26] So great, indeed, were the strains involved in the conference system that, far from being able to go beyond it in the direction of Congresses, states-men attempted to evolve a procedure that was even looser and less binding than *ad hoc* conferences.

In 1838, when the Belgian Conference had resumed in London, Palmerston hoped to use it as a means of reaching a five-Power decision on Mehemet Ali, but he told the Austrian Government that what he wanted was not a conference on that subject, merely 'a concert', and Austria went so far as to agree to 'a concert' but not to a conference. The proposal still foundered on Russian opposition, but in the next year, at the beginning of his effort to secure agreement to a conference on the same question at Vienna, Metternich followed this precedent. He disclaimed the wish for a conference—the word should not be used—and asked only for a concert or a *point d'appui*. Neither the Vienna Conference of 1839 nor the London Conference of 1840–1 were technically regarded as conférences. Though they received suf-ficient authority to be able to give instructions to ambassadors and admirals, they were known as *points d'union* or *points centrals*.[27]

The Concert of Europe suffered under a still more serious limitation. Though conferences met on such questions as Belgium, the Papal states and the Eastern Question—on questions on which, once the Powers could agree among themselves, the business was to impose a settlement on other states—no conference attempted before the Crimean War to impose a settlement on one of the Great Powers or in a question in which a Great Power was deeply involved. At the end of the Austro-Sardinian War of 1848–9 France and Great Britain attempted to assem-ble all the Powers at a peace conference at Brussels to settle the Italian question. It came to nothing because Austria refused to attend unless the Powers declared in advance against territorial changes.[28] There never was a conference on the Italian question. The only conference ever held on the German question was that which assembled to accept

[26] *Ibid.* 174–5.
[27] *Ibid.* 57, 170–3.
[28] Taylor, *op. cit.* 27–8.

in 1852 the settlement between Prussia and Denmark which Palmerston had been left to negotiate alone.

When these strains and difficulties are considered the development of the conference system may seem to have been a far from impressive achievement. But the relevant question is why the Great Powers did not go further still in these last directions and return to the anarchy of the eighteenth century. Their acceptance of the restraints and frustrations of the Concert system was the consequence rather than the cause of their preparedness to be restrained; it was always reluctant and far from complete. But this is true of all international procedure. Though it is often assumed that leagues and conferences are the solution to international conflict, there must be a preparedness to control that conflict before leagues and conferences can be effective; such preparedness is not easy to achieve and is still less easy to maintain. Why were the Powers still prepared to be restrained? Why—and this is a separate question—did their restraint now take the form of permitting the beginnings, if only the beginnings, of formalised international collaboration in the conference system?

The answer to the first question lies partly in the nature of their rivalries. Each was too divided from all the rest, by interest or ideology or both, to permit them to form alliances; yet each was deterred from too much risk alone by the lack of preponderant power. And then to this factor, already at work before 1789, must be added the new fact that the first half of the nineteenth century was a period of continuous internal upheaval in Europe. All the Great Powers were combinations of monarchical and aristocratic institutions. The eighteenth century had shown that monarchs *can* fight each other—as monarchies and republics can collaborate. But now they were all ranged, if in different degrees, against dissidence in their own societies. Before 1830 they had attempted, and failed, to operate the Congress system for the international suppression of disturbances. After 1830 they still found that their rivalries were too great for such cooperation. But from 1830, the year in which revolutions broke out in France, Belgium, Portugal, Spain, Italy, Greece, Poland and the Ottoman Empire, the year in which 'the revolution' stopped halfway, they were at least restrained in their foreign policies by this common peril at home. And so they remained until they realised, after almost continuous unrest, that the revolutions of 1848 had been 'the turning-point at which history failed to turn'. If they would rarely act together against revolution because of their rivalries, they would never act against each other for fear of

encouraging revolution. Frederick William IV of Prussia wrote in 1854:
'I shall not allow Austria, the inconvenient, intriguing, Austria, *to be
attacked by the Revolution, without drawing the sword on her behalf*,
and this from pure love of Prussia, from *self-preservation*.' [29] He was
perhaps alone at that date in still believing in the revolutionary danger;
but his remark fairly sums up the outlook of all the Powers in the
previous generation—and of the Western Powers as well as of the three
Eastern Courts.

France, the Power especially associated with 'the revolution', was
driven in this direction by her rivalry with Great Britain as much as
by her need to avoid driving Great Britain to join the Eastern Powers
against her. In 1847, when she concluded the *entente* with Austria
which she had been seeking since 1833, Guizot told Metternich that
France 'is now disposed and suited to a policy of conservatism . . . a
policy of *entente* is therefore natural to us and founded on the facts'.[30]
His assessment was not belied when, a year later, the French overthrew
monarchy for the last time in a further revolution. Lamartine, the new
Foreign Minister, announced in a 'Manifesto to Europe' that 'the
treaties of 1815 have no legal existence in the eyes of the French Republic'. But one of the aims of the manifesto was to satisfy radical
opinion in France—to avert a more radical revolution there—and for the
benefit of Europe it added that the treaties were nevertheless 'a fact
which the Republic admits as a basis and starting-point in its relations
with other nations'.[31] Lamartine's successors at the Foreign Ministry
went further still. Bastide, later in 1848, would not support the cause of
German nationalism in the dispute with Denmark because 'German
unity would make . . . a power very much more redoubtable to its
neighbours than Germany is today and therefore I do not think we
have any reason to desire this unity, still less to promote it'.[32] Drouyn
de Lhuys, after the re-establishment of the Empire, was always hoping
to drive a wedge between Napoleon III and the Liberal-minded cause.[33]
Napoleon himself presents a problem to historians because, though
sincerely attached to that cause and also anxious to revise the treaties
of 1815 in the interests of France, he could not free himself from the
pressures which, after he had come to power, forced him along with
other governments in the direction of restraint. If European diplomacy
became even more bewildering after 1852 than it had been before,

[29] Quoted in Taylor, *op. cit.* 63 (n.).
[30] *The New Cambridge Modern History*, x, 259.
[31] Taylor, *op. cit.* 5.
[32] *Ibid.* 15–16.
[33] *Ibid.* 65, 70.

this was only partly on account of his unreliability. His unreliability was due to the fact he wanted to advance the liberal-national cause without calling on the spirit of revolution, to revise the treaties without causing a war, to challenge Europe and yet be the champion of order and the *status quo*.

He put the dilemma to the British ambassador soon after becoming Emperor: 'I have every intention of observing these Treaties—but you should recollect how galling they are to France.' [34] He gave this reassurance because he needed the friendship of Great Britain and because Great Britain was more firmly attached to the treaties than any Power—and more firmly attached to them than to any ideological cause. Palmerston was fond of calling himself a pupil of Canning. To begin with he was capable of giving the doctrine of non-intervention a Canningite interpretation—as when, under the terms of the Quadruple Alliance of 1834, he agreed to a French expedition to coerce the Portuguese usurper while opposing any interference by the Eastern Powers. Essentially, however, the policy of actively encouraging the liberal cause against the Holy Alliance died with Canning, and Palmerston, in the priority he gave to the maintenance of the existing treaty system over the advance of the liberal and national causes, was a disciple of Castlereagh. During the revolutions of 1830 and 1848 he took his stand on the treaties of 1815 in resisting popular demands for assistance to the cause of Polish, Italian, Hungarian or German liberation—insisting with Russia on the principle that any changes in the existing treaties would be acts of aggression if they were made without the agreement of the signatories, and departing from the principle of non-intervention only where those treaties,—and British interests—were threatened, as they were by the Prussian attack on Denmark. If it was only in this Schleswig-Holstein dispute that he stood out as the leading opponent of nationalism, he easily accepted its suppression by Russia in Poland and Hungary and by Austria in Italy. He did so in the firm conviction that this was necessary in the interests of 'the political independence and liberties of Europe'.[35] In Italy he hoped, it is true, to persuade Austria to yield and set up an independent kingdom of northern Italy. This was not so much in the interests of the liberties of Italy as from anxiety to anticipate French intervention in Italy and from the belief that Austria, an essential element in the European balance of power, would be strengthened by this policy, as she was being saved by Russian support in Hungary.

[34] *Ibid.* 46–7.
[35] Quoted in *The New Cambridge Modern History*, x, 262.

Palmerston's attitude illustrates how the fear of disorder exerted a powerful effect—as powerful as the material rivalries within the two camps—in bringing about the interpenetration between the Holy Alliance Powers and the Western Powers and the restraint which prevailed among the Great Powers during these years. It was also one reason why, as well as abstaining from reckless policies, the Great Powers developed, however imperfectly, the system of diplomacy by conference. The first new feature of the situation as compared with the second half of the eighteenth century—the fear of revolution—buttressed the effect of a continuing near-equality of power among the leading states in keeping their policies restrained. The second new feature in the situation was that, although the continental Powers remained roughly equal in strength, Great Britain had now moved far ahead of them in power and influence. It is not unreasonable to regard the Concert of Europe as being from one point of view the system which naturally replaced the aim of universal monarchy during the period of British predominance.

Great Britain was now the Power which overtopped all the rest in material strength, occupying in one sense the position previously enjoyed by Austria or Spain or France. Unlike her predecessors she was outside the continent, not in it; and though her primacy was undoubted, it had been built in a period which also saw the rise in absolute strength of several other Great Powers. For these two reasons she was not able and was not tempted, as earlier Powers had been, to associate her power or her security with the submission of Europe to her rule. On the contrary, it was in her interest to keep Europe divided; and this had been sufficient to make her throw her weight against the successful operation of the Congress system. But whereas in the eighteenth century, when she first became powerful, she had become isolationist, profiting from Europe's divisions to advance her position beyond Europe, she now found it possible and desirable both to profit from Europe's divisions and to remain an influence within Europe in order to keep the divisions in check. Canning was tempted to return to the old isolationist policy. Palmerston, the last man to neglect English interests, constantly identified the defence of them with a policy of remaining in Europe in order to preserve the existing international system.

'The interests of England, the preservation of the balance of power and the maintenance of the peace of Europe'[36] was a phrase that was frequently on his lips. Perhaps the chief of those interests for him

[36] *Ibid.* 257.

was 'to guard with care the maintenance of the balance of power', which
would be deranged by 'the attempt of any nation to appropriate to itself
territory which belongs to another nation'.[37] And not only for him. In
1852 Lord John Russell summed up the attitude of all British governments in these days, and also indicated how conference diplomacy had
followed from it. 'We are connected, and have been for more than a
century, with the general system of Europe, and any territorial increase
of one Power . . . which disturbs the general balance of power in
Europe, . . . could not be a matter of indifference to this country, and
would no doubt be the subject of a Conference, and might ultimately,
if that balance was seriously threatened, lead to war.' [38]

If British interests had been differently interpreted the Concert
system could not have developed. But British policy alone could not
have developed it if it had not also responded to the needs and outlook
of the European Great Powers. After the attempt to organise themselves
into a league to suppress revolution had driven them apart, and at a
time when a common fear of revolution merely kept them from being
driven further asunder, they were driven together by yet another new
feature of the times—by the fear of another Napoleon—as well as by
the influence of Great Britain. It was a fear which they shared with
Great Britain; and so much so that as she never hesitated to identify
British interests with the preservation of the existing international
system and both with 'the political independence and liberties of
Europe', 'the general interests of Europe', 'European objects'—to use
more of Palmerston's phrases—so they never questioned that her primacy
did not constitute a Napoleonic danger, that her interests coincided
in this respect with theirs. If all the Powers limited their ambitions
to making London or Vienna or Paris the centre—or to preventing
London or Vienna or Paris from being the centre—of the diplomatic
structure it was because they all knew that they all accepted a conception of Europe which had first been developed by writers in the
eighteenth century, in reaction to acquisitive policies, but never previously practised by governments. They enunciated it in the nineteenth
Protocol of the Belgian Conference in April 1831. 'Chaque nation a ses
droits particuliers; mais l'Europe aussi a son droit. C'est l'ordre social
qui le lui a donné.' [39] It was a conception which represented a retreat
from the Holy Alliance in its insistence on each nation's rights; by its
emphasis on the rights of Europe it invested the balance of power

[37] Quoted in ibid. 258.
[38] Ibid. 267.
[39] Quoted in Webster, op. cit. 65–6.

between the nations with a special significance. Palmerston always spoke of the balance of power not as critics of diplomacy had spoken of it in the second half of the eighteenth century—as incompatible with Europe's 'social order'—but as the essential condition of that order. In his mind it performed this function not merely as the safeguard against an hegemony like Napoleon's. It was this; but it was also the true guide to be followed when changes were unavoidable in Europe's *status quo* and the justification for maintaining that *status quo* as far as possible. It was interchangeable with 'the maintenance of European peace' and the pursuit of 'European objects'. And when he spoke in this way he did so with confidence that all the Powers accepted this equivalence. At this time 'only those who rejected *laissez faire* rejected the Balance of Power—religious extremists at one extreme, international socialists at the other'.[40] But those who accepted *laissez faire* in international relations accepted it within the framework of this theory about Europe.

It was from this theory that the states derived the few principles underlying the conference system: that the Great Powers had a common responsibility for maintaining the territorial *status quo* of the treaties of 1815 and for solving the international problems which arose in Europe; that, when the *status quo* had to be modified or a problem had to be settled, changes should not be made unilaterally and gains should not be made without their formal and common consent; that, since the consent of all was needed, decisions were not to be reached by votes. It was because they all shared this theory that, on the one hand, the refusal to enter into a conference was regarded as evidence of an aggressive attitude—so that the suggestion of a conference was not rejected outright but was avoided by the laying down of unacceptable conditions—and that, on the other hand, the assembling of a conference was not regarded as a diplomatic defeat for those Powers who had been reluctant to attend.[41]

At first sight these principles may not seem any more impressive than the extent to which they were applied in the development of the Concert of Europe. It might be suggested that something like them was, whatever the difficulties, bound to exist between sovereign states disposed to avoid war. Changes to the *status quo* are inescapable in a world of separate Powers. What else could such Powers do but adopt such principles and something on the lines of the Concert system if they did not want to fight—and particularly at this time when they lacked

[40] Taylor, *op. cit.* xx.
[41] Sir Charles Webster, *op. cit.* 66.

the techniques of communication and transport which were subsequently to make constant discussion and contact between them unavoidable, if not always profitable, and yet had been forced into closer contact than had ever existed before? In fact, the principles were more impressive, their application in the Concert system more difficult, than at first appears. To anyone who understands the nature and difficulty of international relations it will not be necessary to emphasise that the Powers could not have adopted and applied them if, over and above the practice of mere restraint, they had not subscribed to some such conception of the international system, and of their place in it, as that which has been described.

THE AGE OF TOTAL WAR *

Raymond Aron

Raymond Aron, French historian, sociologist, and political journalist, is Professor of Sociology at the University of Paris and the author of many books on modern warfare. The most definitive of these is his Paix et Guerre entre les Nations.

Frederick the Great left to his legal apologists the justification of his conquests after they had taken place. Public opinion played hardly any part in the limited warfare of the eighteenth century; the professional soldiers, recruited from the lower classes of society, felt no need to know why they were fighting. In the twentieth century, the soldier and citizen have become interchangeable; and the general public, believing itself peacefully disposed, demands an accounting from its leaders. To prove the enemy responsible for a war has become each government's duty. On each side, historians and intellectuals strive not so much to maintain the morale of the fighting forces alone as to clear the conscience of the whole nation.

The analysis of the origins of the First World War, originally

* "The Technical Surprise" from *The Century of Total War* by Raymond Aron. Copyright 1954 by Raymond Aron. Reprinted by permission of the author and Doubleday & Company, Inc.

based upon the need for propaganda between 1914 and 1918, was carried on, even after the Allied victory, by a sort of revolt against what had happened. Middle-class Europe, proud of its civilization and sure of its progressiveness, regarded war as a monstrosity out of another age. The authors of the Treaty of Versailles demanded reparations, invoking not the defeat in arms, which the vanquished Germans (well aware of what they themselves would have done had they been victorious) would have accepted without demur, but the fact of aggression. The study of the causes of the war was inspired not as much by historical curiosity as by that spirit of moral righteousness. Who were the criminals who had plunged Europe into the abyss of violence? What fortuitous elements had revived the horrors of the past?

Historical research yielded inconclusive results. It did not make an end of uncertainties. Inevitably it disappointed both the pacifists and those who sat in judgment.

The historian, concerned to show the causes of an event, puts two questions, both legitimate, but which must be carefully distinguished. First of all, why did war come at that particular time; and, given the situation, who were the men, or what were the circumstances, that precipitated war? Secondly, how was the situation which led to war created? The first question refers to what are generally called the immediate causes, the second to what are called the remote origins. Historians attribute to the former more or less importance according to their philosophy and also to the results of their inquiry. If they come to the conclusion that the situation led inevitably to war, the immediate causes obviously lost importance.

In their study of the First World War, historians were deeply interested in the immediate causes. The actual events marshaled themselves in a highly orderly fashion. Before the assassination of the Archduke Francis Ferdinand, Europe was living in a state of preparedness, but no one expected an outbreak from one day to the next. Following the assassination, and especially after the Austrian ultimatum to Serbia, chancelleries and populations alike felt the dread of approaching disaster.

A multitude of books and commentaries have attempted to explain the week that passed between July 23, when Austria dispatched her ultimatum to Serbia, and the thirtieth, the day on which Russian mobilization was decreed. Archives have been exhausted, responsible leaders have published their memoirs, and historians have reconstituted the conversations, negotiations, and interviews that had taken place in Vienna, Berlin, St. Petersburg, and Paris. The very accumulation of documents seemed to result in confusion.

More apparent than real, the confusion is based upon three inter-related questions: What were the actions that rendered war not only possible, but probable, and finally inevitable? Up to what point were those actions morally or politically legitimate? What were the intentions of those responsible for them?

No one denies today, as no one doubted then, that the Austrian ultimatum introduced the possibility not only of war, but of general war. The statesmen at Vienna were aware of that risk, just as the German statesmen had recognized it at the discussions in Berlin at the beginning of July. Russia, who regarded herself as protectress of the European Slavs in the Balkans, would not allow Serbia to be crushed or permit her to be transformed from an independent kingdom into a sort of protectorate of the Dual Monarchy. The ultimatum was a challenge to Russia. All Europe realized that the initiative, heavy with menace, had come from Vienna, and that it would not have been taken without the promise of support given in Berlin.

The Serbian reply was moderate in its terms, though it rejected the proposal that Austrian officials participate in an inquiry. If we add to the ultimatum the refusal to accept Serbia's reply, and then the severance of diplomatic relations and the bombardment of Belgrade, we have a succession of acts for which Austrian diplomacy (and indirectly German diplomacy) may be held responsible. This, then, was the European situation in 1914, which made likely the advent of a general war.

Controversy has centered mainly on the legitimacy of the Austrian policy. To what extent did the conduct of the Serbian Government justify what were exorbitant demands under international law? Whatever particular Serbian officials or private politicians might have had to do with the preparation of the Archduke's assassination, the facts known at the time gave no ground for holding the Belgrade Government responsible, and consequently gave the Vienna Government no authority to make demands incompatible with Serbian sovereignty. For the rest, there is little doubt that the Austrian diplomats neither desired nor expected a simple acceptance of their ultimatum. They wanted to "teach a lesson" to the little country that was disturbing its powerful neighbor by supporting or tolerating the "liberation" propaganda of the European Slavs. The men who had determined at Vienna to "teach the lesson" resolutely accepted the possible consequences, including general war.

Thus the real issue is whether we may consider these consequences to have been possible, probable, or inevitable. There is little likelihood of a unanimous conclusion. The historian may ponder the influence of one event on another but his conclusions can never be final. In the present case, one must at least say that the Central Powers had created conditions which rendered war probable. Would its avoidance have required a miracle, or merely more diplomatic patience and imagination in the opposite camp? Speculations on what *might* have happened are endless.

The same sort of controversy was carried on over the Russian general mobilization, the first in date (though, before it became known, the Austrian mobilization had been decided on). Was not that mobilization politically legitimate as a reply to the first operations against Serbia? The German military leaders themselves regarded the Russian mobilization as different in nature from all the other ones because of the time that it required. When that mobilization took place, had not the die been cast, and were not the general staffs in the different capitals impatient to set going a mechanism which left diplomacy no further room for action?

As long as we consider only the two questions of causality and legitimacy, careful inquiry compels us to qualify, but without fundamentally modifying, the Allied contention. It was the Vienna Cabinet that took the initiatives which all Europe has held to be bellicose. It was that Cabinet which threw down the glove to Serbia, and therefore to Russia; it was that Cabinet which wanted a *succès de prestige,* even at the risk of general war. Germany, in giving Vienna a free hand, shared the responsibility, whatever may have been the secret thoughts of her rulers. Even though it were shown that the Entente, and Russia in particular, was too prompt in taking up the challenge, the burden of guilt in the diplomatic sequence of actions and rejoinders would remain with the "initiators."

But such guilt, positive and limited—diplomatic, so to speak—is incommensurable with that imagined by popular passion. Search was made, not for this or that Minister bent on extirpating the Irredentist propaganda of the European Slavs, but for the men who had knowingly embarked on aggression. They were not discovered or, in any case, they were not discovered in the simple guise of storybook villains.

The search for motives or incentives leads to unending controversies. It is possible on the basis of certain testimony to represent German policy as inspired by the desire to launch as soon as possible a war considered to be inevitable. The proposals of Wilhelm II to the King of the Belgians may be adduced, for example. In certain military quarters it was obviously thought that the reorganization of the Russian Army would not be completed until 1917, and that the French forces were short of machine guns and heavy artillery. Such considerations, reinforcing the confidence of the general staff, must have influenced the generals in the discussions at the beginning of July. But the study of archives has revealed a German policy less sure of itself and less definite in its aim. Berlin accepted general war, but it could not be said that the responsible statesmen deliberately set out to provoke it over the Austro-Serbian dispute. That idea certainly crossed the minds of some persons at some moments, but it did not constantly determine the action of the Chancellor, the Emperor, or the Ambassadors.

In other words, when we search for motives the simple picture of aggressors and victims does not stand up to rigorous analysis.

The French statesmen certainly desired war even less. The Tsar and a good many (but not all) of the Russian leaders were afraid of war, perhaps more out of concern for the regime than for the war itself. But the Allies were determined not to tolerate the Austrians' resorting to force in the Balkans, while Viennese diplomacy was no less determined to use force if necessary to gain a *succès de prestige* at the expense of Serbia. On both sides the will to peace was conditional, not absolute. The European situation in 1914 made the localization of the conflict extremely improbable, but both Berlin and Vienna would have been satisfied to attain the immediate objective without starting a general war.

The European scene was not occupied by "sheep and wolf" states, but by sovereign states equally determined to maintain their power and prestige. In Britain and France there was no equivalent of the Pan-Germans or the romantic theorists of violence. Both countries were inclined to be conservative and to renounce dreams of conquest. The Germany of Wilhelm II, actively expansionist, was more inclined to the call of arms than the middle-class democracies. For all that the explosion in 1914 was the result of diplomatic failure.

For a century Europe had enjoyed relative stability. Neither the Crimean War nor the Franco-Prussian War became general. With greater effort the Balkan Wars were brought to an end without irreparable injury to the European equilibrium. The "war monster" that had shaken the Continent from 1792 to 1815 had been chained up. It broke loose again in August 1914.

As soon as we leave the narrow limits of our inquiry into the assassination of the Archduke and the Austrian declaration of war, going back before the crisis of June and July 1914, there is no longer any date that can be regarded as marking the origin of the historical situation that produced the First World War. The Franco-German hostility leads us back at least to the Treaty of Frankfurt, the Russo-German hostility at least to the abandonment of the Reinsurance Treaty by the young Emperor Wilhelm II. But rather than retrace a half century of European diplomatic history, our critical inquiry must restrict itself to the formulation of definite questions.

Any student of the crisis was bound to be struck by the rapidity with which an incident involving an individual prince set all Europe ablaze. Why had the situation become so explosive? Why did so many statesmen and common men alike vaguely sense the rising storm?

The replies of the historians, although differing in detail, are on the whole irresistibly simple, disconcerting to those who want to penetrate beyond the superficial facts and root out the deep-seated forces of which the very participants themselves had no knowledge.

In accordance with an unwritten law of European diplomacy, the very fact of Germany's growth in power provoked a grouping of nations to make a stand against her. The course of the war proved abundantly that the Triple Entente had no surplus of strength over the German-Austrian alliance. But the fact that the Entente was necessary for equilibrium does not explain why it was formed. It had not yet been formed at the end of the last century, though the same considerations had already made it necessary. We must therefore remember simply that the grouping of the great European nations into more or less close alliances was something neither novel nor monstrous that required a special explanation or implied the existence of a culprit.

France, once she had surmounted the consequences of defeat, would normally, in accordance with an old tradition, seek support in the East. It may be that the Franco-Russian rapprochement was facilitated or accelerated by the mistakes of the Wilhelmstrasse. But it would have been difficult, in the long run, for Germany to remain very friendly with both Russia and Austria-Hungary. In preferring the latter she inevitably brought about a rapprochement between Paris and St. Petersburg. As for Great Britain, she was bound to fear a German victory that would eliminate France as a major power and give the conqueror almost unlimited hegemony over the Continent. British diplomacy would perhaps not have heeded the peril to its own profound interests had not the Second Reich, by building a military fleet, de-livered a challenge which the British Empire could not refuse.

For the rest, from the beginning of the century there was a lack of definition in the diplomatic "fronts." Contacts between the courts of Berlin and St. Petersburg were frequent until the eve of the rupture. Wilhelm II tried several times to take advantage of his personal ascendancy over Nicholas II for purposes of high diplomacy. The treaty signed by the two Emperors at Björkö in July 1905, although subsequently rejected by the Tsar's Ministers, must not be forgotten. Until the eve of the catastrophe the relations between London and Berlin, quite apart from dynastic ties, were not those of irreconcilable enemies. As late as 1914 British Ministers had the idea of appeasing German ambitions by negotiating a partition of the Portuguese colonies. In spite of the efforts of French diplomacy, no British Government had entered into any formal engagement: discussions between the general staffs did not interfere with the freedom of decision of the London Cabinet.

The division of the principal nations of Europe into two camps did not necessarily make for war. It only made it inevitable that any conflict involving two great powers would bring general war. From the moment when there was formed in the center of Europe a German empire, industrially foremost in Europe, with a population exceeding that of France by more than fifty per cent, and allied to the Dual Monarchy, a war on the small scale of that of 1870 had become impossible. Neither Russia nor Great Britain would have tolerated a new German victory which would have made of the Reich no longer merely the dominant European state, but a claimant to empire over the Continent.

The two camps were not condemned to mortal combat by any mysterious fatality. The relations between the coalitions had simply deteriorated until clear-sighted observers foresaw the inescapable outcome of armed peace. Who was to blame? The issue has been passionately argued. One side denounced the intolerable manners of Teutonic diplomacy, the demand for Delcassé's dismissal, the spectacular visit to Tangier, the dispatch of a gunboat to Agadir, the annexation of Bosnia-Herzegovina; on the other side it was pointed out that in the course of the half century during which she had been the foremost power on the Continent, Germany had added less to her overseas possessions and profited less by arms or negotiation than weakened France. Germany had made herself intolerable by her brutality, by her arrogance, and by the ambitions of which she was suspected. But under the rules of diplomacy she was not wrong in demanding compensation when France established her protectorate over Morocco. She could not fail to notice that the international conferences were not turning out to her advantage.

The growing tension centered about three principal difficulties: the rivalry between Austria and Russia in the Balkans, the Franco-German conflict over Morocco, and the arms race—on sea between Britain and Germany, and on land between all the powers. The two last causes had produced the situation, the first one kindled the spark.

There are doubtless those who contend that the immediate cause matters little, and that war might have broken out just as easily in 1911 as in 1914. The contention readily suggests itself and is not easily disproven. The fact remains that the Balkan quarrels brought about the actual rupture, just as they had helped to dissolve the pact of conservation which, despite divergent alliances, still united the sovereigns of Russia and Germany. For one thing, the clash between Russia and Austria-Hungary had a diplomatic cause. Repulsed in Asia after her defeat by Japan in 1905, Russia conformed to tradition and redirected her attention and her ambitions to Europe. But, apart from diplomacy, the clash had a deeper cause in the movement of ideas and passions. For two supranational empires still existed in an age of nationalism. The Ottoman Empire had not yet been liquidated, and already diplomats were anxiously anticipating the time when they would have to face the problem of the succession to Austria-Hungary.

Henceforth Viennese diplomacy is more understandable. It was no longer so much a question of avenging the assassination of an Archduke who had favored trialism and whose disappearance pleased many persons in high places. It was a matter of ending once and for all the nationalist propaganda that challenged the existence of Austria-Hungary. Obviously, Russia could not allow the Vienna Government a free hand.

The quarrel between chancelleries interested also the general public in each country. Diplomacy had succeeded in integrating into the Europe which followed the Congress of Vienna a united Germany and a united Italy without a general war. It was unable to perform such a feat again in the twentieth century. The national conflicts in Eastern Europe unleashed general war.

The inquiry into political responsibility carries with it no authority to banish as criminals either men or nations. But inquiry does clarify the significance and the origins of the war. The immediate occasion and the deeper cause largely coincide; for, as we have seen, the reasons for hostility among the various nations of Europe were manifold. The relative strengths and the relationships of alliance excluded partial conflicts. The rise of Germany, whose hegemony France dreaded and whose Navy menaced England, had created an opposition that claimed to be defensive but was denounced by German propaganda as an attempt at encirclement. The two camps alarmed each other, and each tried to soothe its own fears by piling up defensive armaments. The atmosphere grew heavy with multiplied incidents, which spread the conviction of approaching disaster. The explosion finally came in the East, where Russia and Austria were advancing contradictory claims, and where the principle of national sovereignty had ruined the Ottoman Empire and was beginning to undermine the still imposing edifice of the Austro-Hungarian Empire.

Wars are essentially unpredictable. But the wars of the twentieth century have been much more so than were those of the past. The very situations that bring about a modern war are destroyed in its wake. It is the battle in and for itself, and not the origin of the conflict or the peace treaty, that constitutes the major fact and produces the most far-reaching consequences.

It is impossible to recall without a smile the plans drawn up by the French general staff in the period before hostilities began in 1914. They anticipated a daily supply of 13,600 rounds for 75 mm. guns, 465 for 155 mm. guns, and 2,470,000 cartridges for the infantry; a daily production of 24 tons of B powder; 50,000 workers to be employed in 30 factories. The estimated production was to be attained on the eighty-first day after general mobilization. On September 19, instead of 13,600 rounds the general staff asked the Ministry of Armament for 50,000. It obtained that quantity in March 1915, but meanwhile, in January, it had demanded 80,000. This last figure was reached in September 1915, but by then the general staff was demanding 150,000—more than ten times the prewar estimate. This increasing demand for artillery ammunition had its parallel in all other military supplies.

Both in France and in Germany it was expected that the decisive battles would be fought and won within a few weeks. Peacetime reserves of equipment and munitions would suffice, it was thought, for the operational needs requisite to victory. The result, in France, of this remarkable optimism was that on September 15, after thirty days of operations, stocks were half depleted, and the arsenals held no more than 120,000 rounds for 75 mm. guns. If in October the peacetime reserves had not been exhausted virtually at the same moment on both sides, lack of ammunition might have brought to one or the other the decision vainly sought in the field. During the first two years, guns of one caliber were kept supplied only at the expense of guns of other calibers. Not until 1917 did production more or less fulfill the constantly increasing requirements of the battlefield. Instead of 50,000 employees, 1,600,000 were engaged in defense plants, and to these workers should be added those in the United States employed directly or indirectly in the Allied war effort. Ministers and their military advisers thought they were undertaking a war "like any other," expecting its issue to be determined by a few battles of annihilation. Instead, they had committed the people of their countries to a long trial by attrition. Between the aspiration and its fulfillment there intervened what I propose to call the "technical surprise."

In the last century the American Civil War had offered a fairly good preview of what we call total war, with regard particularly to the relentless mobilization of national resources and the competition over the new inventions.[1] The period of European peace between 1871 and the Balkan Wars had been marked by rapid progress in armaments. The underwater mine, the torpedo, and the submarine revolutionized naval tactics. On land, the universal use of the semiautomatic rifle and of the carbine, the perfecting of the machine gun, and the adoption of rapid-fire artillery gave unprecedented firepower to armies of greatly increased manpower.

Finally "technical surprise" came as the climactic element of an evolution in which the wars of the French Revolution and Empire represent an important stage, if not actually the beginning. National wars are fought by the people as a whole, and no longer by professional armies; the stakes are no longer dynastic interests or the fate of a province, but the future of the collective society or its ideals. In the epoch of democracy (that is to say, of compulsory military service) and of industry (i.e., of mass production and destruction), national wars naturally tend to expand into total wars. What needs to be explained is not how the war of 1914 spread across the Continent and became "hyperbolic,"[2] but the fact that the nineteenth century was able to escape a similar outcome to the French Revolution and the industrial revolution.

[1] "In the Civil War in America the rifled gun came more and more to the fore. Yet, from the armament point of view, the main characteristic of this war was the extraordinary inventiveness displayed throughout it. During it the magazine-loading rifle and a machine gun were invented. Torpedoes, land mines, submarine mines, the field telegraph, lamp and flag signalling, wire entanglements, wooden wire-bound mortars, hand-grenades, winged grenades, rockets and many forms of booby traps were tried out. Armoured trains were used; balloons were employed on both sides. Explosive bullets are mentioned, searchlights for 'stink-shells' to cause 'suffocating effects' were asked for. The use of flame-projectors was proposed and the U.S.S. Housatonic was sunk on February 17, 1864, by a small man-propelled Confederate submarine." J. F. C. Fuller, *Armament and History* (New York: Scribner, 1945), pp. 118–19.

[2] The term "hyperbolic" war was first used by Pareto.

Europe had been spared in the nineteenth century by a streak of good fortune. Diplomacy was able to localize the conflicts because none of them definitely threatened the general balance of power. Neither the victory of Great Britain and France over Russia, nor that of France over Austria, nor that of Germany over Austria and, subsequently, over France, appeared to endanger seriously the onlooking powers. These events modified the balance established at Vienna, but did not destroy it. And none of them threatened the economic or social regime of any of the warring countries. The wars were limited both in regard to the resources employed and to the issue at stake, and they did not arouse ungovernable popular passion. They were fought mainly by professional armies (except for the second phase of the Franco-Prussian War). The general staffs, wedded to their habitual methods, were slow in making use of new weapons. The superiority of infantry weapons contributed largely to the Prussian victory in 1866, as did the superiority of artillery (breech-loading instead of muzzle-loading guns) to that of 1870. The brutality of the initial successes in 1866 and in 1870, due to the disparity of military organization, armament, and fighting strength, prevented any resort to a strategy of attrition and the progressive mobilization that is its normal result. But such good fortune could not be repeated indefinitely.

After 1815 the principal European powers, whether out of wisdom, fear of the "monster," or obedience to tradition, had returned to the professional army. Only Prussia had maintained conscription, and she had won the foremost place in Europe. No one could fail to learn the lesson. All the nations, beginning with France, bitter in her defeat, conformed to the logic of democracy and re-established compulsory military service. The general staffs remained, on the whole, conservative. Obliged to modernize rifles and machine guns and field artillery, they made mistakes, especially the French staff, as to the strategic and tactical implications of the new weapons. They failed to grasp certain lessons of the Russo-Japanese War and the Balkan Wars, underestimated the machine gun, and almost entirely ignored the air arm and the role of the internal combustion engine. But in spite of all this, in 1914 the nations rose in arms supplied by modern industry and went out to do battle. Hyperbolic war could have been averted only by a lightning victory of one side or the other. That possibility was removed by the Battle of the Marne, and the die was cast.

It is often contended that decisive results are impossible because of the democratic and industrial structure of modern armies. Nothing can be more mistaken, as we now know, than to imagine armies of millions of men to be essentially incapable of dealing a mortal blow, to be doomed to clash and wear each other away where they stand. The events of June 1940 dissipated that illusion. If the German Army had had the tactical and organizational superiority over the French in August 1914 that it had in June 1940, it would have gained the day as quickly; and for some years or decades the potentialities of total war would have remained unknown in Europe. Greater numerical strength, which the German general staff could have obtained by further drafts from the Eastern front, might very well have been 'sufficient. In short, the conditions for total war were present: all that was needed for its development was an opportunity, which in this case was offered by the approximately equal strength of the opposing forces.

Through an accidental and transient condition of warfare, which affected the West especially, total war, for four years, limited itself to the trenches. Defensive techniques were superior to offensive, so that by accumulating formidable firing power, it became possible to pulverize. the enemy's front lines without too much difficulty; but the terrain won was so broken up that it became in itself an obstacle. Enemy defenses, improvised by hastily assembled reinforcements, halted the attack, which could not be supported by an artillery paralyzed by its lack of mobility and the effects of its own fire.

Until 1917 the intensification of warfare was mainly quantitative. The cry "More guns, more shells!" had a meaning that went beyond propaganda. Month after month, in offensive after offensive, more and more guns were massed and more and more rounds were fired. When there were not enough guns at the front, the artillery preparation went on for several days—giving the enemy time to prepare his resistance. Later the duration was reduced and the intensity increased. In the Somme offensive in 1916, there were 900 heavy guns and 1,100 light guns massed along 10 miles of front.[3] Neither side was able to win a decisive battle. Every breach in the line was more or less quickly filled. After initial successes, the offensive petered out. Even during the latter months of 1918, when the Allies were considerably superior in men and matériel, they were able to strike heavy blows against the German Army, but there was no victory of annihilation.

Quantitative extension of warfare obviously does not prevent what might be called qualitative extension, recourse to new arms and new tactics. The French Army possessed about one hundred airplanes in August 1914, and several thousand by 1918. The use of motor vehicles

[3] At Stalingrad, in January 1943, the Russians massed 4,000 guns along 4 kilometers of front, i.e., 1 gun per meter of front.

for transport, of wireless communication, of armored tanks, gradually transformed the methods of operation, especially after 1917. But whatever share in the successes of the Allies may be attributed to tanks, essentially the war was brought to an end by means of the same arms with which it began. Machine guns and artillery, partly in improved models but mostly in larger numbers, completed the task they had begun. The new arms—aircraft and tanks—were not yet dominant, but they had shown that they would be in the next war.

Total war, as it took place in 1914–18, with problems of supply, strategy of attrition, stable fronts, and field fortifications, left the public with a horrifying memory of tens of thousands of soldiers sacrificed to conquer a few square miles, the inhuman life of the trenches, the crushing and startling technical superiority of arms, organization, and production over personal qualities—all of which helped dissipate the traditional romanticism of warfare and nourish revolt. Or rather, revolt against war, as old as humanity, was to be reinforced by revolt against war machines, a revolt comparable with the first revolt of craftsmen against industrial machines. But as long as the struggle continued, that latent revolt had to be repressed and enthusiasm maintained.

Thus the "technical surprise" is among the main causes of the geographical extension of war and the growth of wartime passions.

The extension of the war in Europe took a classical form. In the event of a conflict between great powers, said Machiavelli, the small ones generally have no chance to remain neutral, and nothing to gain by doing so, for their attitude arouses the enmity of the conqueror, whoever he may be; whereas if they take sides they may get into the good graces of the distributors of booty. The successive interventions of Turkey, Italy, Bulgaria, and Rumania were preceded by negotiations in conformity with tradition. Each of the major opponents exerted itself to secure a fresh ally by offering gains which ordinarily neither owned. The result of these competitive promises was usually determined in advance. Italy's aspirations could only be satisfied at Austria's expense. Great Britain and France had no difficulty in parading a generosity that Germany could match only by sacrificing her comrade in arms. On the other side, the Central Powers rallied Bulgaria, who coveted Serbian territory, whereas it was in Serbia's defense that the Allies had drawn their sword. Needless to say everyone's choice was determined by other considerations as well—a gamble on the result of the fighting, moral affinities, popular feeling, and so on.

In any case, none of these European interventions greatly increased the initial scale of hostilities or decisively modified the balance of power. Japan seized the opportunity to appropriate some strategic positions held by the Germans. Only the American intervention represents an unprecedented fact and marks a historic date, whose retrospective significance is very clear. That intervention was essentially due to the technical amplification of the war. The provocation was, of course, the German Government's declaration of unrestricted submarine warfare in violation of an agreement made several months earlier in Washington. The new technique of naval warfare, contrary to international law as understood at the time [4] (as was the British long-range blockade), precipitated the decision of the United States and thereby assured the defeat of the Second Reich.

There has subsequently been an attempt to minimize the validity of the provocation. During the isolationist period there was criticism of the bankers and industrialists who had supplied the Allies with credit, equipment, or raw material and who were now afraid, it was alleged, of losing their money or their customers. But such an interpretation, implying capitalist machinations, would, even if true, refer us back to the same reality. Even the Anglo-French alliance lacked the means to bring the total war to an end. The United States had been involved economically in the struggle before becoming militarily involved, because the joint resources of the British and French empires were insufficient to maintain the monstrous lethal machine.

Still other commentators claim that the submarine warfare was merely a pretext, and that the American leaders simply recognized at the time of that menace that British control of the seas was indispensable to the United States. American security would be endangered if Great Britain were defeated; a virtually hostile power would rule the Old World and be free to extend its domination, or at least its enterprises, across the oceans. But one may very well ask if the Americans would have recognized their solidarity with Great Britain had submarine warfare not shaken the ascendancy of the Home Fleet, revealed the German naval potential, and produced a general apprehension of a peace dictated on the scale of the war itself, that is to say, a Carthaginian peace.

At the same time we must not overlook the part played by sentiment or ideology. In critical moments the kinship of Britons and Americans

[4] When the United States entered the Second World War, the naval staff ordered unrestricted submarine warfare. The war technique that had aroused indignation twenty-five years earlier was now accepted as normal.

dissipates mutual misunderstandings, resentments, and irritations. By inscribing on its banners the sacred words Democracy and Freedom, the Entente aroused general sympathy in America. Since it was universally inspired, the language used by the Allied representatives was understood in every continent. A crusade to make the world "safe for democracy" was, so it seemed, of world-wide concern. What meaning had the defense of German *Kultur* outside of Germany itself?

It was ideology that won over American opinion to participation in the war, arousing and maintaining the enthusiasm of a young nation. The fundamental consideration, nevertheless, was primarily materialistic. The Allies had sought American aid to help support the burden of the hyperbolic war. Economic participation became military partnership when the submarines tried to break the bond already existing between the European and American democracies, and so threatened to leave a navy regarded as hostile ruling the oceans and separating ancient Europe from the New World.

There has been incessant inquiry into the origin of the First World War, but no one has ever asked why it became hyperbolic. Did the people of different countries fight to the death because they detested each other, or did they detest each other because they fought so furiously? Did the belligerents set themselves unlimited objectives from the outset, or did they acquire those objectives in proportion to the increase in violence? Was it passion that produced the technical excess, or technical excess that fomented passion? Not unreservedly or without qualification, and fully recognizing the interaction of the two phenomena, I would maintain that the motive force of the evolution at that time was technical. Technique it was that imposed the organization of enthusiasm, condemned to failure the efforts at conciliation, drove out the old diplomatic wisdom, and contributed to the spread of the crusading spirit, finally producing a peace that created the situation from which the second war started.

The start of the first war was marked in all countries by an explosion of national fervor. Patriotism overrode social resentments and revolutionary aspirations. In a few days, sometimes in a few hours, the socialists, who had been pitiless critics of the diplomacy of both the Wilhelmstrasse and the Quai d'Orsay, were carried away by the collective enthusiasm and embraced the popular sentiment. National unity was established at once in France against German aggression and in Germany against the Russian peril.

The German victories during the first weeks redoubled the fighting spirit of the Germans and steeled the resolution of the French. German terrorism and atrocities (which Allied propaganda exaggerated but did not invent), far from depressing the morale of the French, aroused a sort of fury, nourished by both military tradition and the "pacifist" revolt against the horrors of war.

As the sterile process of slaughter continued with no sign of an early end, enthusiasm waned and social claims, repressed by the sudden surge of ancestral passions, disrupted this national unity. Though neither side would give way, resolution was succeeded by resigned persistence, fervor gave place to reluctant acceptance. Propaganda and ideology usurped the place of genuine feeling.

At first both were adapted mainly to the needs of the country behind the lines. As a rule the combatants were killing one another without contempt or hatred. At times they felt bound together by a mystical communion of fate. Even when they hated, they hated a being of flesh and blood, the enemy whom it was necessary to kill so as not to be killed. The abstract hatreds that are ravaging our century are the work of urban masses, not of soldiers at the front. What Elie Halévy called "organized enthusiasm" forms a chapter in the history of civil mobilization. The need was desperately obvious: it was essential to maintain the nation's unity and will to fight. Defeat must be made to appear catastrophic, victory an unmixed blessing. In other words, the stake at issue escaped definition by the rules and regulations of diplomacy. It was no longer a question of shifting frontier posts a few miles. Only sublime—and vague—principles, such as the right of peoples to self-determination or "the war to end war," seemed commensurate with such violence, sacrifice, and heroism. It was technical excess that gradually introduced ideologies in place of war aims. Both sides claimed to know what they were fighting *about,* but neither said what it was fighting *for.*

Once general war had started, its provocation was bound to be forgotten, and the stake no longer had anything in common with the cause. All past relations between the European powers were reviewed and challenged. The chancelleries discovered forgotten grievances and ambitions in their files, the people in the memories.

Secret diplomacy was given free play. The British Ministers accepted Russia's claim to Constantinople, the French secured recognition of their claims in Alsace-Lorraine. The great powers signed with Italy, Rumania, and Serbia secret agreements that were not all indefensible but promised a sharing of booty rather than a peace in conformity with principles. It was easier to proclaim that the war was being fought in defense of freedom than to publish the results of such negotiations, which were interconnected and sometimes contradictory.

The same is true of the other side. At the time of its first victories, the German Government had not made known the conditions it would impose on the vanquished. But influential private associations, from the industrial groups to the Pan-German League, broadcast the most grandiose projects. Should they annex Belgium or merely require guarantees? Should they appropriate only France's colonial empire or part of her continental territory as well? The leaders of the Central Powers were also hoping for total victory; they, too, refused to bind themselves in advance by any formal announcement of their war aims. They, too, left it to the intellectuals to define the "ideas of 1914" in whose name Germany was carrying on the war for the defense and glory of her unique *Kultur*.

After two years of war, it may be that some of the German leaders, and even those of Austria-Hungary, would have been glad to return from "war ideologies" to "war aims," to silence the tumult of propaganda and allow the diplomats to speak again. But it was too late. A vague note was dispatched on December 1916 to which the Entente replied on January 10, 1917, with a note that was not precise on every point but which, by suggesting the liberation of the Czechs, seemed to imply the disintegration of Austria-Hungary. In July 1917, the German Parliament adopted a motion in favor of a peace without annexations or indemnities, but the Entente was not prepared to accept. The secret negotiations with the Emperor Charles of Austria for a separate peace collapsed, and everyone turned again to await the outcome of the battle.

From 1914 to 1918 there were special obstacles to a compromise peace. The strategic situation was temporarily favorable to the side that had the lesser chance of final victory. A war can be cut short when the side whose superiority is established on the battlefields shows moderation and renounces some of the gains that might come from victory, in order to save itself the trouble of bringing the enemy to his knees. Germany had won the first successes, and the fighting had taken place outside her territory. For all that, as the fighting went on she became the probable loser, so greatly did the resources of the Entente, which was mistress of the seas, come to exceed those of the Reich, suffocated by the blockade. In other words, according to the actual battle maps, Germany had the advantage; but according to the soundest predictions, the Entente would win in the end. In such a case, neither side could afford to make any important concessions.

Yet, quite apart from what might be called this element of chance, it was peculiarly difficult to end by negotiation in the traditional way a war that had become a war of peoples and of ideas. Nobody had started a crusade in 1914, nobody then was out to liberate oppressed nationalities, to make an end of secret diplomacy, or to spread democracy. To win sympathy in the world, and to maintain the morale of their suffering nations, governments resorted to ideology, and that element played an important part in the Allied conduct of the war from the time of the American intervention and the Russian Revolution. The war had not been started in order to bring about the triumph of particular views of life and society; but as the cost of operations mounted these views were felt to be essential to inflate the prospective profits of victory. It was declared that the peace would be durable only if it were dictated unconditionally after crushing the enemy. The demand for total victory was not so much the expression of a political philosophy as a reflex reaction to total war.

TOTALITARIAN DIPLOMACY *

Gordon A. Craig

Gordon Craig is Professor of History at Stanford University. He has written extensively on German history and is editor of The Diplomats, *a major comparative study of modern diplomacy.*

In a treatise that is justly admired by students of diplomacy, François de Callières wrote in 1716: 'The art of negotiation . . . is so important that the fate of the greatest states often depends upon the good and bad conduct of negotiations and upon the degree of capacity in the negotiators employed. . . . It is not necessary to turn far back into the past to understand what can be achieved by negotiation. We see daily around us its definite effects in sudden revolutions favourable to this great design of state or that, in the use of sedition in fermenting the hatreds between nations, in causing jealous rivals to arm against each other so

---

* From Gordon A. Craig, "Totalitarian Approaches to Diplomatic Negotiation," in A. O. Sarkissian, ed., *Diplomatic History and Historiography* (London: Longmans, Green & Co. Limited, 1961). Reprinted by permission of Gordon A. Craig.

that the *tertius gaudens* may profit, in the formation of leagues and other treaties of various kinds between monarchs whose interests might otherwise clash, in the dissolution by crafty means of the closest unions between states: in a word, one may say that the art of negotiation, according as its conduct is good or evil, gives form to great affairs and may turn a host of lesser events into a useful influence upon the course of the greater.' [1]

Since these words were written, changes in the methods of communication, in the nature of international society, and in the distribution of political power within the states that comprise it have profoundly affected the forms and the techniques of diplomatic negotiation; but its importance as an instrument of national power has in no way been diminished. There is no easier way to demonstrate this than to consider the role of negotiation in the history of the totalitarian states of the first half of the twentieth century. The failure of the Fascist and National Socialist governments to understand or take advantage of the uses of negotiation was not the least important cause of the difficulties that in the end overwhelmed Italy and Germany; whereas the Soviet regime's ability to devise new techniques of negotiation and to adapt traditional ones to its own purposes carried it through the hazards of the inter-war period and, after the Second World War, consolidated and expanded the position won by Soviet arms.

I

The deficiencies of Fascist diplomacy and the amateurishness of its leaders' ventures into negotiation may be explained, in part at least, by the fact that the first years of Mussolini's political life were spent as a journalist. The talents that are required to make a man a good newspaperman are different from those that one expects to find in a competent diplomat. Cavour is one of the rare individuals who have possessed both kinds, and Mussolini, in this and other respects, was no Cavour. The Duce's newspaper experience left him with a tendency to be preoccupied with style rather than with substance, with a hankering after sensational strokes and dramatic coups that would look good in headlines, and—although this hardly accords with that cynicism that newspapermen are traditionally supposed to possess—with an excessive regard for newspaper opinion and a dangerous sensitiveness to newspaper criticism.

[1] *The Practice of Diplomacy*, being an English rendering of François de Callière's 'De la manière de négocier avec les souverains', presented with an introduction by A. F. Whyte (London, 1919), pp. 7, 16.

Mussolini's fundamental attitude toward diplomacy, and the attention he paid to its purely verbal aspects, were bound up, in a curious way, with his editorial policy for *Il Popolo d'Italia*. He once explained how he had impressed upon that journal, 'in thousands of articles, headlines, drawings and sketches inspired by me, a polemical and aggressive character, one of continual battle'; [2] and, after he became chief of state, he seemed to feel that it was only fitting that this should become the characteristic mark of every aspect of Fascist policy, including foreign policy. He was forever talking about 'the Fascist style' which he equated with courage, resolution, action, forcefulness, dynamism. 'Note that I do not love the hesitant and conventional form', he said in December 1925. 'I affirm'.[3]

This dislike of the hesitant and the conventional extended to those forms of diplomacy which sought, with a minimum of public display and a maximum of deliberation and reflection, to solve European problems in the first postwar decade, as well as to the frequent attempts made, at Geneva and elsewhere, to reach collective agreements by means of multilateral negotiation. All of these were, in a phrase frequently used by the Duce's son-in-law, 'contrary to our diplomatic style'.[4] Mussolini's prejudice against multilateral negotiation can probably be traced back to the chastening experiencing of his first diplomatic venture, when, at the Lausanne Conference of November 1922, his *gaucheries* were received by the other delegates with an amusement that bordered on scorn.[5] But there can be little doubt that it was rooted also in his belief that the satisfactions to be gained from collaborative diplomacy in the interest of general appeasement were not worthy of Fascist Italy, which must dazzle the world with spectacular triumphs of its own.

During the first decade of his regime, however, Mussolini could not afford, and did not attempt, to base his policy upon these prejudices. The defiant, and only partly successful, stroke at Corfu in August 1923 [6] was not imitated in the years that followed; and, if Mussolini was prone to ringing declarations of imminent action, he generally allowed the word to stand for the deed. Thus, in February 1926, when he electrified Europe by a clear threat of military action north of the Brenner unless an end was made to criticism of his policy in the South Tyrol by the Austrian and German parliaments, he backed down quickly when the Austrians proposed to bring the matter before the League of Nations,

[2] Herman Ellwanger, *Sulla lingua de Mussolini* (Verona, 1941), p. 22.
[3] Benito Mussolini, *Scritti e discorsi* (Milano, 1934-9), vol. V, pp. 321 ff.
[4] Galeazzo Ciano, *L'Europa verso la catastrofe* (Verona, 1948), p. 338.
[5] See Harold Nicolson, *Curzon: The Last Phase* (London, 1934), pp. 288 ff.
[6] See Gaetano Salvemini, *Prelude to World War II* (New York, 1954), pp. 44 ff.

delivering a second speech in which, behind 'a characteristic parade of truculence', he converted his earlier menaces into 'an inoffensive intimation that he would defend himself if attacked by others'.[7]

Throughout these early years, the exigencies of domestic policy reduced Mussolini's dynamism to what has been called a 'random and unco-ordinated striking-out in all directions in the hope of scoring points on the cheap'.[8] The best that can be said of it is that it did no real harm to Italy's basic interests, since Mussolini was content to leave the bulk of the diplomatic business of the state, which was, as elsewhere, carried on by the continuous negotiations that go on in embassies and foreign offices, in the hands of the professional foreign service and the permanent officials in the Palazzo Chigi. By making concessions to their leader's vanity, these officials were able to moderate his outbursts and control his ambitions, while cementing relations with those Powers, like Great Britain, who were willing to respect Italy's traditional interests and even to assent to modest increases in her influence in Africa and eastern Europe.[9]

All of this changed when the deterioration of economic conditions in the early 1930s, and the consequent disruption of European power relationships, opened new vistas to Mussolini's eyes and made him impatient with old restraints. The dismissal of Grandi as Foreign Minister in July 1932 marked the inauguration of a new policy of all-out revisionism and, simultaneously, the beginning of that decline of the influence of the professionals in Italian diplomacy that was to reach its nadir in the Foreign Ministry of Galeazzo Ciano.[10] As their role diminished, negotiation became almost a forgotten art in the Italian service, a tendency encouraged by the belief that the goals Italy now sought must be attained not by diplomacy but by heroism.

Even the atmosphere of conventional courtesy that customarily reigns in the diplomatic corps and is conducive to the useful exchange of views was dispelled by Ciano. Once he had become Foreign Minister, he seems to have determined to realize his father-in-law's stylistic ideals and insisted that Italian diplomats must henceforth make their behaviour reflect the approved *tono fascista*.[11] The meaning of this phrase is elusive; it seems to have meant a proud and militant bearing that would impress the foreigner with the dignity and strength of the new Italy.

[7] A. J. Toynbee, *Survey of International Affairs*, 1927 (Oxford, 1929), p. 199.
[8] H. Stuart Hughes, 'The Early Diplomacy of Italian Fascism', in *The Diplomats, 1919–1939*, edited by Gordon A. Craig and Felix Gilbert (Princeton, 1953), pp. 224 ff.
[9] *Ibid.*, pp. 216 ff.
[10] See especially Felix Gilbert, 'Ciano and his Ambassadors', in *The Diplomats*, pp. 512 ff.
[11] Raffaele Guariglia, *Ricordi, 1922–1946* (Napoli, 1950), p. 193.

Its practical effect was to make ambassadors dispense with traditional forms and usages of polite intercourse (Ciano insisted on the deletion of even the most conventional expressions of good will from ambassadorial declarations),[12] to be constantly on the alert for slights to Italy's honour, to adopt a hectoring tone in delivering communications and complaints to the governments to which they were accredited, and, in general, to conduct themselves, especially in countries that were not bound by ideological or more formal ties to Italy, as if they were in an enemy camp.

This made it virtually impossible for envoys abroad to perform effectively their duties of representation, reporting and negotiation. Representing Italian interests seemed now to consist for the most part of continual protestation against criticisms of Fascism, even when they were made by private citizens; and this, as one Italian diplomat noted, was ludicrous, when one remembered that Fascist Italy was 'all too prone to criticize, injure, jeer at, and menace all the peoples of the world, and not in private conversations, but in manifestations of an official character and in articles in a press which the whole world knew was rigidly controlled by the government'.[13] Ambassadorial reporting degenerated into demonstrations of conformity to Fascist style; and the reports from posts like Belgrade, Sofia, and Bucharest in the last years of the peace contained little of interest except descriptions of the ambassadors' success in bullying their hosts.[14] Finally, the possibilities of ambassadorial negotiation of any kind were handicapped, not only by this new cult of bad manners, but also by the apparent belief in the Palazzo Chigi that, in certain capitals—Paris, for example—an attitude of disdainful reserve was all that should be expected of a Fascist diplomat. 'What ought I try to accomplish in Paris?' asked Guariglia as he left for his post in November 1938. 'Nothing,' answered Ciano. 'It will be difficult', the ambassador replied, 'but I will do my best.'[15]

The subordination of diplomacy to the *tono fascista* was even more patent in the negotiations that Ciano carried on personally at Mussolini's orders. In these he appears to have been more interested in the speed with which an agreement could be reached and the publicity that could be garnered from it than in anything else. In general, his negotiations were amateurish in technique and dangerous in result.

The best illustration of these failings is to be seen in the negotiations

[12] *Ibid.*, pp. 255 ff.
[13] Emanuele Grazzi, *Il principio della fine* (Roma, 1945), p. 13.
[14] Ministro degli Affari Esteri, *I documenti diplomatici italiani* (Roma, 1952 et seq.), 8th series, vol. XII, nos. 100, 177, 672, 819.
[15] Guariglia, *op. cit.*, p. 357.

for the Pact of Steel of May 1939, 'this fatal error', as Guariglia calls it, 'of inauspicious memory'.[16] The reasons for seeking a military alliance with Germany were in themselves hardly compelling. There is strong reason to believe that Mussolini was goaded into abandoning his earlier reserve by scornful articles in the French press about Italo-German friction,[17] although he may have been moved also, as Italian and British diplomats have argued, by a desire to replace the loose Axis tie, which gave Italy no control over her German associate and no right to be consulted by her, by a formal treaty which gave her both these things.[18] However that may be, the way in which the pact was negotiated on the Italian side was nothing short of slipshod. Mario Toscano has pointed out that the most inexcusable aspects of Ciano's conduct were his willingness to leave the actual drafting of the treaty of alliance entirely to the Germans, and his failure, during the talks with Ribbentrop in Milan, 'to discuss or even to set limits on the general nature of its contents'.[19] As for Mussolini, while his Foreign Minister was placing this dangerous degree of trust in German intentions, his sole interest was apparently to have the pact proclaimed in the press even before its terms were worked out, presumably to put an end to the gibes in Paris.

Some time later, when he handed the draft treaty to Ambassador Attolico in Berlin, the Director of the Legal Department of the German Foreign Ministry told him that 'the Foreign Minister [Ribbentrop] considered that the draft corresponded completely with what he and Count Ciano had recently agreed and that, therefore, it presumably did not require any more negotiations on the final version'.[20] Since there was no clear definition, in either the Italian or the German record of the Milan talks, of what had been agreed upon there, it was difficult to contest this; [21] and, in any case, the Italian government seemed too eager for ratification to haggle over amendments. When Ciano and General Pariani came to Berlin at the end of May, some minor changes, based

---

[16] *Ibid.*, p. 395.

[17] Mario Toscano, *Le origini del Patto d'Acciaio* (2nd ed., Firenze, 1956), p. 308.

[18] Massimo Magistrati, *L'Italia a Berlino, 1937–1939* (Verona, 1956), pp. 348 ff.; *Documents on British Foreign Policy, 1919–1939*, edited by E. L. Woodward and Rohan Butler (London, 1949 et seq.), 3rd series, vol. V, no. 598. ('Mussolini has bought the right to be consulted by Hitler, and the price is the pact.' Sir Percy Loraine.)

[19] Toscano, *op. cit.*, pp. 318 ff.

[20] *Documents on German Foreign Policy 1918–1945: From the Archives of the German Foreign Ministry* (Washington, 1949 et seq.), series D, vol. VI, no. 371. Hereafter cited as *German Documents*.

[21] Toscano, *op. cit.*, p. 339.

on suggestions of Attolico, were made; [22] but the final document was nevertheless dangerously imprecise.[23]

Unlike most treaties of military alliance, the Pact of Steel included no definition of the *casus foederis,* no escape clauses, no stipulation of necessary consultation. There was not even a secret protocol defining German intentions; and the promise that no war was contemplated for three years, which had been requested by the Italians, was purely verbal and was not intended to be kept, as Ciano was to discover in his talks with Hitler and Ribbentrop at Salzburg in August 1939. On the other hand, the treaty so precipitately negotiated by Ciano was, as far as Italy's obligations were concerned, rigid and unconditional; and, unless Mussolini was prepared to repudiate his pledge, in case of German action of which he disapproved, Italy was bound to fight at a time of Germany's choosing. Moreover, the Germans were protected against any real possibility of Italian withdrawal by Mussolini's concern over what the newspapers wrote about him. Events were to show that, even when Hitler agreed in August 1939 to Italy's abstention from immediate hostilities—an agreement won in part by the skilful way in which Attolico presented Italy's deficiencies in materials and weapons [24]—the Duce was not content. Smarting under charges that he had broken his word, he led his country into a war for which she was neither materially nor psychologically prepared.

Given Mussolini's temperament, this might have been impossible to prevent in any case; but it was facilitated by the nature of, and the obligations imposed by, the Pact of Steel. All in all, it can hardly be denied that the neglect and misuse of negotiation deprived those Italians who desired peace in 1939 and 1940 of weapons with which to combat the vanity and impulsiveness of their leaders.

II

In retrospect it would seem that the weakness of Italian diplomacy arose from the essential frivolity of the officials charged with the task

[22] Magistrati, *op. cit.,* pp. 344 ff.

[23] See the text in *German Documents,* series D, VI, no. 426. Ferdinand Siebert has written: 'Seldom indeed in history has an alliance been concluded which, despite all its fine talk about cohesion, ideological kinship, and solidarity was based—thanks to the levity of one partner and the disingenuousness of the other—on so many ambiguities and imprecisions as the German-Italian Pact of Friendship and Alliance of May 1939.' 'Das deutsch-italienische Stahlpact,' *Vierteljahrshefte für Zeitgeschichte,* 1959, p. 390.

[24] *Documenti diplomatici italiani,* 8th series, XIII, nos 293, 298, 304, 307; Magistrati, *op. cit.,* pp. 432 ff.; Galeazzo Ciano, *Diario* (Roma, 1946), I, p. 150; *German Documents,* series D, VII, nos. 307, 308, 317.

of conducting it; and, behind Ciano's shocked protest, upon learning in August 1939 of Hitler's intention of going to war, that 'no indication had been given by Germany, either in the conversations at Milan, or in the talks during his visit to Berlin, that the situation in respect of Poland was so grave,' [25] lies a pathetic admission that he had not mastered the art of negotiating even with his own allies.

Adolf Hitler can hardly be accused of Ciano's kind of *leggerezza*. He both understood what could be gained by negotiation and, at various times in his career, demonstrated his ability to use it, in ways of which Callières would have approved, 'in the dissolution . . . of the closest unions between states' and 'in the formation of leagues . . . between monarchs whose interests might otherwise clash'. His faults as a states-man are, therefore, of a different order from Mussolini's. He is to be criticized, not for lack of diplomatic proficiency, but rather for the fact that he refused to be content with the great gains that negotiation could bring to his country, but sought greater ones in war.

Despite the suspicion with which he was viewed by professional diplomats when he came to power, Hitler showed considerable facility in the use of diplomatic means during his first years. In the unfolding of his policy, there was, for one thing, little of the incoherence that had characterized Italian policy in the 1920s. Hitler was aware that the revisionism and expansion upon which his heart was set could be pursued only after the home front had been stabilized and Germany's armed forces built up. While the *Gleichschaltung* was being carried out, therefore, and the Versailles Treaty undermined, the Führer encouraged foreign states to believe that his government would effect no radical break with the policy of the past. This he did, in the first place, by retaining the existing Foreign Ministry staff and by relying on diplo-mats who were known abroad and whose continued employment would have a reassuring effect.[26]

In the second place, unlike Mussolini, Hitler was not given to com-plicating the work of his diplomats in the field (whose task, essentially, was to explain away the brutalities of his domestic programme and to portray him as a force for European order) by inveighing against the international *status quo*. His public pronouncements at this stage were pacific, disarming, even ingratiating, designed to divert foreign atten-tion from his real intentions and to blunt criticism of, or split possible opposition to, his policies, by promising concessions or hinting at will-

[25] *German Documents*, series D, VI, no. 43.
[26] Karl Dietrich Bracher, 'Das Anfangsstadium der Hitlerischen Aussenpolitik', *Vierteljahrshefte für Zeitgeschichte*, 1957, pp. 69–70.

ingness to make agreements desired abroad.[27] Hitler realized that the
public statements of heads of government were not the least important
of modern channels of negotiation, and he showed great skill in using
this means of advancing his purposes and supporting the efforts of his
envoys at Geneva and foreign posts. It was by this means that he was
able, after his withdrawal from the Disarmament Conference and the
League of Nations in October 1933, to mislead the other Powers by his
professed willingness to consider any schemes of arms limitation that
they might propose; and this channel was also used with effect in
persuading states which criticized his withdrawal from the collective
security system to enter bilateral negotiations with him.

In the last-mentioned area of negotiation, Hitler's first years were
marked by two successes that were admirably designed to protect him
from collective counteraction as his policy evolved. These were the pact
with Poland, which drove a wedge into France's eastern alliance
system,[28] and the Anglo-German naval agreement of June 1935, which
split the Stresa Front and destroyed the last possibility of reprisals for
Hitler's violations of the arms clauses of the Versailles Treaty.[29] The
notable feature of these examples of 'dynamic' diplomacy is that there
was nothing impulsive about them. The possibility of a treaty with
Poland seems to have been in Hitler's mind as early as April 1933; [30]
in September he instructed his Foreign Minister to talk with his Polish
opposite number about 'the best means of creating a better atmosphere
in the relations between the two states'; and in November he authorized
the formal negotiations that eventuated in the treaty of 26 January
1934.[31] The idea of a pact with Britain had interested Hitler for an even
longer period, stretching back before his coming to power; and, after he
became Chancellor, he took it up and played an important role in push-
ing the naval negotiations to a successful issue. His private talks with
Lord Allen of Hurtwood in January 1935, with the British Ambassador
in February, and with Sir John Simon in March, and his public address
of 21 May 1935 certainly made a more important contribution to the

[27] A good example is Hitler's speech of 17 May 1933 concerning Germany's
stand on disarmament. See *The Speeches of Adolf Hitler*, edited by Norman H.
Baynes (Oxford, 1942), II, pp. 1041–1058.

[28] Richard Breyer, *Das Deutsche Reich und Polen, 1932–1937* (Würzburg,
1955), pp. 106 ff., and 113.

[29] See, for instance, the speech of 21 May 1935 in *The Speeches of Adolf
Hitler*, II, pp. 1218–1246.

[30] Herbert von Dirksen, *Moskau, Tokio, London: Erinnerungen und Betracht-
ungen zu 20 Jahren deutscher Aussenpolitik, 1919–39* (Stuttgart, 1950), p. 123.

[31] Republic of Poland: Ministry for Foreign Affairs, *Official Documents concerning Polish-German and Polish-Soviet Relations, 1933–39* (London, 1940),
pp. 11–24; *German Documents*, series C, II, nos. 84, 87, 88, 217, 218, 219.

pact's conclusion than the tactics used by Ribbentrop when he led the German delegation to London in June.[32]

After the middle of 1935, when Germany's growing military might supplied an authoritative backing for her diplomacy, Hitler was never again as dependent upon negotiation as he was in his first years; and, after 1936, when he was given his first proofs of the weakness and indecision of the western democracies, his tendency was to rely more upon military pressure than upon negotiating skill and persuasiveness. The tone of German diplomacy now began to change; Hitler's public statements on foreign policy became menacing; and, especially after Ribbentrop became Foreign Minister in February 1938, the style of Foreign Ministry communications became peremptory and sometimes arrogant.[33] Ribbentrop himself had such an exalted conception of his role that he was led to indulge in astonishing displays of bad manners when he felt that his dignity had been hurt.[34] Aside from this, he had no real sympathy for genuine negotiation. As Attolico once said, he could see nothing but his own version of the facts;[35] he had no patience with lengthy deliberations, being desirous of headlong decisions;[36] and he was interested, not in agreements of mutual advantage, but only in settlements that were imposed upon his *vis-à-vis,* or treaties of alliance that were directed against third powers.

These traits were not considered as weaknesses by Ribbentrop's master who had now lost his own interest in negotiation and the benefits it might bring. By the end of 1937, as the minutes of his conference with his generals on 5 November reveal,[37] he was thinking of triumphs that could be won only by the sword; and negotiation had become the handmaiden to war. The change of attitude is clearly seen in the instructions given to Konrad Henlein, the leader of the Sudeten German party, who was ordered, as he pursued his negotiations with the Czech government, to set his claims so high that the Czechs would rather fight

[32] See W. Malanowski, 'Das deutsch-englische Flottenabkommen vom 18. Juni 1935 als Ausgangspunkt für Hitlers doktrinäre Bündnispolitik', *Wehrwissenschaftliche Rundschau,* 1955, p. 416; D. C. Watt, 'The Anglo-German Naval Agreement of 1935; an Interim Report'. *Journal of Modern History,* 1956, pp. 157, 159 ff.

[33] This change was apparent even in the language of professionals like Ernst von Weizsäcker, the Under Secretary. See the language in which he 'categorically refused' to accept a French protest after the Prague coup of March 1939. *German Documents,* series D, VI, no. 20.

[34] See Paul Schmidt, *Statist auf diplomatischer Bühne, 1923–1945* (Bonn, 1949), pp. 457 ff.

[35] *Documenti diplomatici italiani,* 8th series, XII, no. 503.

[36] Ernst L. Presseisen, *Germany and Japan: A Study in Totalitarian Diplomacy 1933–1941* (The Hague, 1958), pp. 198, 208.

[37] *German Documents,* series D, I, no. 19.

than accept them.[38] The same point of view determined Hitler's own tactics as the Polish dispute came to a head a year later. The Führer seems to have been genuinely concerned lest the Poles decide to accept the terms that they had rejected in March 1939 or lest they, or someone else, submit counter-proposals that might compel him to accept a compromise short of war. To prevent this, he not only declined the good offices of third powers,[39] but refused to allow his ambassadors to Poland and Great Britain, who were on leave in Germany, to return to their posts.[40] On 22 August 1939, Hitler openly admitted his preference for violent solutions by saying to his generals: 'Now Poland is in the position in which I wanted her . . . I am only afraid that at the last moment some swine or other will yet submit to me a plan for mediation.' [41]

The irrationality that prompted this insistent refusal of present advantage and this fateful trust in the uncertain promises of war was to recur in June 1941, when Hitler declared war upon the Soviet Union. The declaration followed a period of twenty-two months in which the Nazis had won tremendous concessions from Moscow by a combination of negotiation and subtle menace, and during which the Soviet Union had yielded on every contested point of the partition of eastern Europe that had been stipulated in Hitler's most spectacular diplomatic stroke, the agreement with the Soviets in August 1939. It has been said that in those twenty-two months 'the Soviet Union had gone to greater lengths in appeasing Germany than the British and French governments had gone during the period between Hitler's advent to power and 15 March 1939'; [42] and it was not certain that the limits of that appeasement had yet been reached.[43] Yet Hitler the warrior had superseded Hitler the negotiator; and even the knowledge that Great Britain was still unsubdued did not dissuade him now from transforming the conflict in which he was already engaged into a two-front struggle that would in the end destroy his country.

[38] *Ibid.*, series D, II, no. 107.

[39] *Survey of International Affairs, 1939–1946: The Eve of War 1939,* edited by Arnold Toynbee and Veronica M. Toynbee (London, 1958), pp. 342 ff. and 377.

[40] *German Documents,* series D, VI, no. 674; VII, nos. 2, 32, 82; Carl W. Schorske, 'Two German Ambassadors', in *The Diplomats,* pp. 509–510.

[41] *German Documents,* series D, VII, no. 192.

[42] *Survey of International Affairs, 1939–1946: The Initial Triumph of the Axis,* edited by Arnold Toynbee and Veronica M. Toynbee (London, 1958), p. 365.

[43] As late as 28 April 1941 the German Ambassador in Moscow was sure that the Soviet government was 'prepared to make even further concessions'. *Nazi-Soviet Relations, 1939–1941,* edited by R. J. Sontag and James S. Beddie (Washington, 1941), p. 332.

III

In sharp contrast to Hitler's approach to negotiation is that of the Soviet Union. Far from preferring the arbitrament of war to decisions made at the council table, the Soviets have generally valued diplomacy for its ability to win great triumphs at small risk and have shown virtuosity, not only in mastering its procedures and forms, but also in devising formidable negotiating techniques of their own.

In the first stages of the Soviet experiment, there was, it is true, some tendency to regard diplomacy as an outworn bourgeois institution, and Leon Trotsky actually spoke of shutting up the Foreign Office completely.[44] This mood soon passed, and, from the days when G. V. Chicherin led a top-hatted and striped-trousered delegation to the Genoa conference of 1922, the Soviet Union has made full use of all the possible channels of diplomatic negotiation and shown complete command of the time-tested methods of the profession.[45] The official Soviet history of diplomacy says proudly: 'Soviet diplomacy is master of its technique. In its relations with foreign Powers, it defends the interests of its country in the most worthy manner; and, with an incontestable authority and with impeccable special skills, it conducts negotiations and concludes agreements advantageous to its country.' [46]

One need only think of some of the diplomatic successes won at moments when the Soviet Union was vulnerable to outside pressure, or threatened by outside attack, to admit the justice of this. In the first ten years after the Bolshevist revolution, the Soviet Union often faced the possibility of complete diplomatic isolation. It escaped this by its success in persuading England and other countries to enter negotiations for trade agreements, by the subsequent treaties of recognition concluded with the major Powers, by continuous negotiation in areas like Afghanistan, the Middle East and Poland for protective or diversionary purposes, and by the masterful cultivation of the association with Germany that was inaugurated so sensationally at Rapallo in 1922 and confirmed by the Treaty of Berlin in 1926.[47] These successes were won

[44] Theodore H. von Laue, 'Soviet Diplomacy: G. V. Chicherin, Peoples Commissar for Foreign Affairs', in *The Diplomats*, p. 235.

[45] A number of western studies of diplomacy, including Sir Ernest Satow's *Guide to Diplomatic Practice*, and Jules Cambon's *Le Diplomate*, were translated into Russian in the interwar years and used in training courses.

[46] V. P. Potemkin *et al.*, *Histoire de la diplomatie* (Paris, 1946–47), III, p. 787.

[47] The latter treaty in particular played a part in the initiation of the negotiations that led to the Nazi-Soviet pact in August 1939. See *German Documents*, series D, VI, nos. 406, 490, 579, 607.

for the most part by patient negotiation and the skilful use of the techniques of classical diplomacy, especially the art of playing upon the differences of other powers or appealing to their greed or their apprehensions. In the use of the traditional arts of bargaining, Soviet negotiators, in these early days and later, showed themselves the equals of their adversaries, sometimes to the surprise of the latter; [48] and in preparing their case before the opening of negotiations, in mastering the agenda and the technical aspects of items included on it, and in tactical adroitness in exploiting the legal aspects of existing agreements which bore on current negotiations, they sometimes showed an embarrassing superiority of performance, as the first post-Second World War meetings of the Foreign Ministers showed all too clearly. [49]

Despite the excellence of their training in the external forms of diplomacy, and their skill in using it, Soviet negotiators have always had a fundamentally different approach toward diplomacy from that of their western colleagues. To them diplomacy is more than an instrument for protecting and advancing national interest; it is a weapon in the unremitting war against capitalist society. Diplomatic negotiations, therefore, cannot aim at real understanding and agreement; and this has profound effects upon their nature and techniques. [50]

For one thing, it means that not all of the negotiations entered into by the Soviet government are intended to eventuate in settlements, a fact that irritates or baffles some western diplomats and seems to repre-

[48] Thus, during the negotiations for American recognition of the Soviet Union in November 1933, the British Ambassador in Washington could write: 'M. Litvinov has proved somewhat of a surprise to the State Department. I learn on good authority that he has been showing himself the toughest of negotiators. He has evinced no trace of any ambition to achieve a personal success. He has had the blandest, but firmest, of retorts ready for any question, and has appeared quite ready to depart empty-handed at any moment.' *British Documents,* 2nd series, VII, no. 542. Speaking of Molotov's conversations in Berlin in November 1940, Paul Schmidt wrote: 'Molotov had a certain mathematical precision and unerring logic in his way of speaking and presenting arguments. In his precise diplomacy he dispensed with flowery phrases and, as though he were teaching a class, gently rebuked the sweeping vague generalities of Ribbentrop and, later, even of Hitler.' *Statist auf diplomatischer Bühne,* p. 516.

[49] Newspaper reports of the meeting of Foreign Ministers in London in 1945 would seem to bear this out. See, more recently, 'Topics of the Times', *New York Times,* 26 July 1959; and John Foster Dulles, *War and Peace* (New York, 1950), pp. 27 ff.

[50] See Stephen D. Kertesz, 'Diplomacy in the Atomic Age', *Review of Politics,* 1959, pp. 132 and 193; and 'American and Soviet Negotiating Behavior' in *Diplomacy in a Changing World,* edited by Stephen D. Kertesz and M. A. Fitzsimons (Notre Dame, 1959), pp. 144 ff.

sent a complete denial of the purpose of diplomacy.[51] Negotiations may
be begun, or agreed to, by the Soviets, not as a means of promoting
agreement on an issue, but of delaying it, pending the clarification of
problems in other areas or the successful completion of other talks.
They may be started out of mere speculation, as a means of eliciting
the views, defining the interests, or testing the tenacity of the parties
on the other side. They may be designed for purely propaganda purposes, as 'elaborate stage plays' to edify and win the sympathy of the
uncommitted part of the world.[52] Because of this, as Philip Mosely has
written, the first task of the diplomats who engage in talks with Soviet
negotiators is to try to discover whether the latter have instructions
to negotiate seriously or, indeed, have any instructions at all, beyond
a general directive to make propaganda for the Communist cause.[53] If
they do not, the result is apt to be what a British Foreign Secretary
has described, in a moment of exasperation, as 'negotiation by
equivocation.' [54]

Even when Soviet diplomats have been instructed to seek a settlement, the subsequent negotiations are apt to diverge in marked respects
from the rules that have traditionally guided diplomatic intercourse in
the western world. Soviet diplomats do not subscribe to Callières's belief
that there exists between negotiators a *commerce d'avis réciproque*.[55]
Bound themselves by rigid directives that allow little flexibility they
cannot understand the freedom of manoeuvre permitted to western diplomats. Moreover, since they regard their opposite numbers as ideological
enemies, they are bound to view all their moves, however trivial, with
suspicion [56] and to regard any means that promise to win advantage
over them as legitimate.

These things being so, negotiations with the Soviets have generally

[51] 'I have "done" many conferences in my life but never went into one without
some hope of a fairly quick result. No one could say the same today. Results are
often not expected, and often not even desirable. . . .' Lord Vansittart, 'The
Decline of Diplomacy', *Foreign Affairs*, 1950, p. 184.
[52] Henry A. Kissinger, 'Reflections on American Diplomacy', *Foreign Affairs*,
1956, p. 46.
[53] Philip E. Mosely, 'Some Soviet Techniques of Negotiation', in *Negotiating
with the Russians*, edited by Raymond Dennett and Joseph E. Johnson (New
York, 1951), p. 274.
[54] Selwyn Lloyd, describing Gromyko's tactics during the London talks of
July 1959, *New York Times*, 22 July 1959.
[55] *The Practice of Diplomacy*, pp. 20–21.
[56] Writing of Molotov's behaviour at the London meeting of the Foreign
Ministers in 1947, Herbert L. Matthews said: 'He is innately suspicious. He seeks
for hidden meanings and tricks where there are none. He takes it for granted that
his opponents are trying to trick him and put over something nefarious.' *New York
Times*, 7 December 1947.

been marked by an almost automatic Soviet opposition at the outset to all proposals from the other side of the table, followed by persistent and uncompromising advocacy of the Soviet point of view. The tactic of initial rejection extends to the most innocuous suggestions made by the partner in negotiation, since the Soviets apparently believe that 'the trivial is the first line of defence on which to meet the enemy assaults that always aim at the crucial'.[57] In September 1929, when Arthur Henderson presented M. Dovgalevsky with a list of questions that he felt should be discussed and settled before the resumption of diplomatic relations between their two countries, the Soviet representative came to the second meeting with a list of his own, with the questions in quite a different order, and proceeded to fight, with a zeal out of all proportion to its object, for his arrangement.[58] This sort of thing has been normal practice and has come to be expected by western negotiators.

The stoutness with which the Soviets hold to their own proposals has become proverbial. 'Anyone accustomed to dealing with M. Litvinov', Sir Esmond Ovey wrote from Moscow in December 1929, 'will remember how he frequently appears to be on the point of agreeing to suggestions made to him, but in practice, when pressed for any definite statement, he invariably reverts to his original point of view.'[59] Similar statements have been made in more recent times about the persistence of Molotov and Gromyko.[60] Nor has this inflexibility in negotiation been easily shaken by non-diplomatic means. It is true that, in the years 1940 and 1941, during the almost continual Soviet-German negotiations about the disposition of eastern Europe, the Soviet Union was forced repeatedly to yield to German gains, in face of *faits accomplis* backed by the threat of force.[61] But in the inter-war years and in the period since 1945, other cases of this are hard to find; and attempts to bring non-diplomatic pressure to bear on the Soviets, far from succeeding, have sometimes merely given them an opportunity to claim loudly and publicly that they were being threatened by imperialist Powers. When the British government sought in 1933 to intimate in private negotiations that they would break off economic relations unless the Soviets released British engineers who were accused of wrecking and espionage, the Soviet government replied with press releases claiming 'gross external pressure' and persisted in their course.[62]

The granting of concessions in the hope of eliciting concessions in

[57] Nathan Leites, *A Study of Bolshevism* (Glencoe, Ill., 1953), pp. 55 ff.
[58] *British Documents*, 2nd series, VII, no. 20.
[59] *British Documents*, 2nd series, VII, no. 43.
[60] See Sidney Gruson's remarks on Gromyko's negotiating style, in *New York Times*, 26 July 1959.
[61] See *The Initial Triumph of the Axis*, pp. 319 ff., 364 ff.
[62] *British Documents*, 2nd series, VII, no. 306.

return has had no more effect in persuading Soviet negotiators to modify their positions. In the fruitless Anglo-French negotiations with the Soviet Union in the summer of 1939, the western governments repeatdly conceded points described by the Soviet negotiators as being of fundamental importance, hoping that this would facilitate agreement, only to discover, once they had done so, that new points were now of fundamental importance to the Russians, whose intransigence was in no wise diminished. This led Lord Halifax to question the genuineness of the Russian desire for a treaty and to complain to the Soviet Ambassador that 'the Soviet Government had not budged a single inch, and we had made all the advances and concessions. Saying "No" to everything was not my idea of negotiation.' [63] In the years since 1939 other diplomats have learned, as the British did then, that yielding points, or even changing one's original position for reasons other than the presentation of new evidence, merely encourages the Soviets to hold fast.[64]

Soviet inflexibility is generally combined with the skilful use of tactics designed to wear out the patience or weaken the judgment of their adversaries. Among these tactics is the use of bad manners, not out of personal or ideological vanity, which was responsible for the discourtesies of Ribbentrop and Ciano, but with the calculated intention of disconcerting their partners in negotiation, throwing them off balance, and thus betraying them into ill-advised decisions. It was a convention of the old diplomacy that one pretended not to notice the artifices employed by one's adversary and accepted the verbal formulas with which he covered them.[65] The Soviets have no patience with this kind of tolerance. 'I may be mistaken', said Sir Anthony Eden at the Moscow conference of Foreign Ministers in 1943, 'but . . .' 'You *are* mistaken', Molotov interrupted harshly, breaking the thread of Eden's argument and destroying its effect.[66] By this kind of crude attack upon the rules of elementary courtesy and by false accusations, name-calling and the imputation of the worst possible motives to their adversaries, Soviet negotiators have been able on occasion to obscure the real issues at stake, to divert the course of discussion to subsidiary points, and even to bully a conference into accepting their point of view. Deliberate assault upon the values and forms of the old diplomacy is a means by which the Soviets seek to impose their views and their standards on the rest of the world, and they have not been entirely unsuccessful.[67]

---

[63] *Ibid.*, 3rd series, VI, no. 135; *The Eve of the War, 1939*, p. 454.
[64] John N. Hazard in *Negotiating with the Russians*, p. 46.
[65] See François Walder, *Saint-Germain ou la negoçiation* (Paris, 1958), p. 110.
[66] Philip E. Mosely in *Negotiating with the Russians*, pp. 283 ff.
[67] See Lord Strang, *Home and Abroad* (London, 1956), p. 206.

The most successful Soviet tactic is their use of time. Kurt Schumacher once said to an American diplomat, 'The day you Americans are as patient as the Russians, you will stop losing the cold war.' [68] American negotiators, and western diplomats in general, have found it difficult to learn this lesson and have sometimes, in their anxiety for a happy conclusion to talks, seized upon illusory concessions or grasped at dangerous 'agreements in principle' in order to be able to claim a success.[69] This weakness is something the Soviets are constantly watching for; and, because they are free from parliamentary or public pressure, they are usually able to hold their ground calmly, while insinuating into the foreign press charges that their adversaries are needlessly protracting negotiations. Since they have often been dealing with democratic countries in which there are parties or pressure groups sympathetic to the Soviet Union, these tactics have frequently been effective.

The practice of prolonging negotiations for months and even years, coupled as it sometimes is with a shifting of the centre of negotiation from the ambassadorial to the ministerial level and from there to the level of heads of state, often has the effect of blurring the outlines of the issues at stake and making less precise the original points of difference. The Soviets make the most of this by issuing press communiqués which are designed to confuse the general public and which often impute to their opponents views that weaken their position while strengthening the Soviet case. This kind of tactics was used with effect in the repeated and protracted negotiations in the 1920s over the question of the Russian debts and enabled the Soviet Union to avoid payment without penalty. A more recent example of their use was afforded when, at the end of his visit to the United States in 1959 and his talks with the President about the Berlin problem, Premier Khrushchev informed the press that he was satisfied that the President recognized that the existing situation in Berlin was 'abnormal'.[70] The President may indeed have used this term, for the Western Powers have never denied the abnormality of the Berlin situation, while attributing it to the failure to unite Germany. He did not, however, mean to suggest that this abnormality could be corrected by withdrawing Western

---

[68] Charles W. Thayer, *Diplomat* (New York, 1959), p. 96.

[69] A good example is afforded by the attitude of the Labour Party during the Anglo-Soviet trade negotiations in 1924, when they were so eager for agreement that they forced the Foreign Office to accept an unworkable formula. See Philip Viscount Snowden, *An Autobiography* (London, 1934), II, pp. 680–6. See also remarks of John Foster Dulles before the National Press Club in January 1958. *Department of State Bulletin*, 3 February 1958.

[70] Max Frankel in *New York Times*, 30 September 1959.

troops from the city or altering its status to the advantage of the East German regime, although this was what Khrushchev implied. But so many talks had been held on the subject since the original Berlin note, and in so many different places and with so much publicity, that it was not easy for newspapermen to detect the distortion immediately; and, once it had been printed, it could be cited, and has since been cited, as a significant American admission of the fundamental weakness of the western position in Berlin. One of the main tasks of those engaged in negotiations with the Soviet Union consists in keeping the record straight, so that it can be revealed to the public at any time without tactical disadvantage to them,[71] and so that their position will not be eroded by unwitting concessions imposed on them by imputation.

These techniques of negotiation helped protect the Soviet Union in its most vulnerable years, defended its interests in the period before the outbreak of the Second World War, and won from its Allies more than adequate compensation for the losses it suffered in that war. But these have not been the only effective weapons in the Soviet diplomatic armoury; and, in a more thorough analysis of Soviet negotiating be-haviour, attention would have to be paid to other methods that have helped consolidate the war-time gains and now threaten to expand them. These would include the new methods of economic diplomacy, which have been used with undeniable success by Soviet negotiators of agree-ments for technical assistance and aid to underdeveloped countries,[72] and the various techniques of public negotiation, with particular reference to their use in the United Nations.[73] Even in a brief account it can be noted that the Soviet Union has effectively emulated Hitler's use of the public statement as a means of negotiation and has employed the exchange of letters between heads of state for the same purpose. Indeed, it might almost be said that by these means the Soviet Union has been able to be a party to negotiations·to which she has not been invited, for, by timely use of threats against NATO members,[74] of proposals for disengagement of Soviet and Allied troops from central Europe,[75] or of invitations to summit conferences,[76] she has forced the periodic meetings of the NATO Council to discuss *her* views, *her* policies, *her*

[71] On this, see Thayer, *op. cit.*, p. 98.

[72] Klaus Knorr, 'Ruble Diplomacy', *Memoranda of the Center of International Studies* (Princeton, 1956).

[73] See Kertesz in *Review of Politics*, 1959, p. 376.

[74] Editorial, 'Soviet Atomic Diplomacy', *New York·Times*, 28 March 1957; editorial, 'Soviet Campaign', *ibid.*, 13 December 1958.

[75] See Gordon A. Craig, 'Germany and NATO', in *NATO and American Security*, edited by Klaus Knorr (Princeton, 1959), pp. 254 ff.

[76] *Department of State Bulletin*, 2 June 1958, pp. 906 ff.

proposals rather than their own, and to spend time and energy combating the divisiveness promoted within the alliance by her tactics.

IV

Some years ago, when Sir Harold Nicolson delivered his Chichele Lectures on the evolution of diplomatic method, he said: 'I have not observed that . . . the Soviet diplomatists and commisars have evolved any system of negotiation that might be called a diplomatic system. Their activity in foreign countries or at international conferences is formidable, disturbing, compulsive. I do not for one moment underestimate its potency or its danger. But it is not diplomacy: it is something else.' [77]

There are doubtless many who would agree with Nicolson in lamenting the decline of the older diplomacy and in refusing to consider the Soviet Union's way of conducting international relations as diplomacy at all; [78] but the question of nomenclature need not be debated here. What is clear is that the Soviet approach to negotiation has been less impulsive, more systematic and more effective in its results than that of either Italian Fascism or German National Socialism. In an age when war is no longer acceptable as a continuation of policy by other means, and when the importance of reaching settlements short of war is undeniable, the Soviet methods of negotiation would appear to deserve as much study by western diplomats as their own diplomatic tradition has received from their professional colleagues within the Soviet Union.

[77] Harold Nicolson, *The Evolution of Diplomatic Method* (London, 1954), p. 90.

[78] 'Diplomacy could flourish only so long as there was a loose, tacit and general agreement to behave *more or less* like gentlemen.' Vansittart in *Foreign Affairs*, 1950, p. 185. It is interesting to note that Adolf Hitler, at least before he came to power, felt a fundamental incompatibility between Soviet and Western diplomacy. In 1932 he wrote: 'I look upon . . . Soviet diplomacy not only as being unreliable but, above all, as being incapable of being considered of the same nature as the foreign political activity of other nations, and, in consequence, as being something with which one cannot negotiate or conclude treaties.' Thilo Vogelsang, ed., 'Hitlers Brief an Reichenau vom 4. Dezember 1932', *Vierteljahrshefte für Zeitgeschichte*, 1959, p. 434.

PREVENTIVE DIPLOMACY *

Inis L. Claude, Jr.

Inis Claude, Professor of Political Science at the University of Michigan, has written two highly respected studies of international politics and organizations: Swords into Plowshares *and* Power and International Relations.

I

It has been widely assumed and frequently asserted that the United Nations was originally intended and expected to function as the institutional manager of a full-fledged collective security system, capable of bringing collective force to bear against any aggressor. In most instances, this assertion is made in the context of a discussion of the failure of the United Nations to realize that ideal. Sometimes the founders of the Organization are convicted of idealism; they should have known better than to expect the United Nations to be effective as an instrument of collective security. Sometimes an objective analysis of the changes which have occurred in the setting within which the Organization operates is presented as explaining the failure of the collective security scheme; thus:

The great-power split, together with the admission of large numbers of African, Asian, and European neutralist states, has almost destroyed the collective security functions that were to be the organization's principal reason for existence.[1]

More often, the Soviet Union is pictured as the villain in the piece; by abusing the veto power and obstructing the creation of the enforcement mechanism envisaged in Article 43 of the Charter, it has frustrated the realization of the promise of collective security.[2] Whatever the ex-

---

* From Inis L. Claude, Jr., "The Management of Power in the Changing United Nations," *International Organization,* **XV** No. 1 (Winter, 1961), pp. 223–35. Reprinted by permission of the editor.
[1] Thomas J. Hamilton, "The Changing United Nations: Morale Lowered by Deadlocks," *New York Times,* December 30, 1960.
[2] See Eisenhower's letter to Bulganin, January 12, 1958, reproduced in Paul E. Zinner, ed., *Documents on American Foreign Relations, 1958* (New York:

planatory argument, the essential point in such statements is that the United Nations was intended to be, but has failed to become, the directing mechanism of a universally effective collective security system.

Why has it been so generally assumed that the establishment of the United Nations represented an effort to institutionalize collective security in the postwar world? An attempt to answer this question must precede an assessment of the validity of the assumption itself.

In the first place, it may be suspected that this interpretation of the United Nations experiment was reached by the processes of elimination and deduction from a preconceived definition of the purposes of general international organization. Was the new world order designed as a balance of power system? Certainly not. Participants in the creation of the United Nations were too emphatic in their criticism of reliance upon balance of power, and too insistent in their assertion that they were creating a system better than balance of power, to permit that interpretation. True, they did not whip the balance of power as vigorously and persistently as their Wilsonian ancestors had done a generation before, but that was presumably because they thought it uneconomical to spend their time in flogging a dead horse. In any case, the United Nations was essentially a new version of the League of Nations, and it was well understood that the latter organization had been conceived by men who repudiated the balance of power system and aspired to introduce an alternative system. If the projected scheme were not a balance of power system, was it then a world government? No, it was clearly much more modest than that. If proof were needed, one could refer to the Moscow Declaration of October 30, 1943, in which the major powers of the anti-Axis coalition had declared the purpose of "establishing . . . a general international organization, based on the principle of the sovereign equality of all peace-loving states," [3] or to President Roosevelt's decisive assertion that:

> We are not thinking of a superstate with its own police forces and other paraphernalia of coercive power. We are seeking effective agreement and arrangements through which the nations would maintain, according to their capacities, adequate forces to meet the needs of preventing war and of making impossible deliberate preparation for war and to have such forces available for joint action when necessary.[4]

Only one of the standard categories remained. If the United Nations

---

Harper, 1959), p. 89; see also, Sir Leslie Munro, "The Case for a Standing U.N. Army," *New York Times Magazine,* July 27, 1958, p. 27.

[3] *A Decade of American Foreign Policy, Basic Documents, 1941–49,* Senate Document No. 123, 81st Congress, 1st Session (Washington, 1950), p. 12.

[4] *Postwar Foreign Policy Preparation 1939–1945,* Department of State Publication 3580, General Foreign Policy Series 15 (Washington, 1949), p. 269.

were not designed to implement the concepts of balance of power or world government, then who could doubt that it must be an experiment in collective security? This conclusion must have come easily to men who stressed the resemblance of the new Organization to the defunct League. The original general international organization had been dedicated to the effectuation of collective security. It was natural to assume that the second edition was dedicated to the same purpose.

Secondly, it must be noted that the entire process of planning and formulating the United Nations Charter was dominated by the theme: "We are going to create a collective security system, and this time we are going to make it work." The United States planners were preoccupied with the necessity of providing the new Organization with an enforcement mechanism which would enable it to effectuate the collective security principle by coercive means which had been denied to the League.[5] In the opening sessions of the San Francisco Conference, a long procession of speakers reiterated the proposition that statesmen had gathered to create a world organization which could and would maintain the peace, by force if necessary. A typical expression of the prevailing viewpoint was provided by Joseph Bech, speaking for Luxembourg, who declared that the peoples of the world

would not forgive their leaders if they returned to a policy of balance of power, which would inevitably result in a race for armaments heading straight for another war. The protection of peace can only be insured on the basis of collective security.[6]

Moreover, the end of the conference was marked by exultant speeches proclaiming the initiation of a real collective security system. Joseph Paul-Boncour of France declared that "the international organization will no longer be unarmed against violence. . . . That is the great thing, the great historic act accomplished by the San Francisco Conference. . . ."[7] The venerable Jan C. Smuts said of the Charter:

It provides for a peace with teeth; for a united front of peace-loving peoples against future aggressors; for a united front among the great powers backed by the forces of the smaller powers as well. . . . And it provides for central organization and direction of the joint forces for peace.[8]

Thus, the assumption that the creation of the United Nations sig-

[5] See Ruth B. Russell and Jeannette E. Muther, *A History of the United Nations Charter* (Washington: Brookings, 1958), pp. 3, 4, 206, 209, 227–228, 395, 557.

[6] UN Information Organizations and U. S. Library of Congress, *Documents of the United Nations Conference on International Organization* (New York, 1945), I, p. 502.

[7] *Ibid.*, p. 668.

[8] *Ibid.* p. 678.

naled a new effort to institute a universal collective security system was encouraged. In view of the circumstances, it is hardly surprising that this interpretation gained general acceptance. Nevertheless, it is fundamentally incorrect, as a careful analysis of what the world's statesmen did at San Francisco and a more extensive review of what they said about their handiwork, will indicate.

The crucial element in the analysis is an understanding of the import of the veto rule which enables any of the five permanent members of the Security Council to block decisions on substantive matters in that organ—including the determination that aggression has taken place, the designation of the guilty party, and the decision to resort to sanctions, military or otherwise, against the aggressor. Such decisions, be it noted, are fundamental to the operation of a collective security system. The veto rule clearly gives each of the great powers the capacity to prevent the operation of the United Nations enforcement system against itself, against any state which it chooses to support and protect, or in any other case in which it prefers not to participate or to have others participate in an enforcement venture under United Nations auspices. The veto provision, in short, renders collective security impossible in all the instances most vital to the preservation of world peace and order, and problematical in cases of lesser importance.

It will not do to say that the founding fathers of the United Nations went home from San Francisco with the blissful assurance that they had formulated a beautiful system of collective security, only to be rudely shaken later by the discovery that the system was spoiled by a devilish Soviet Union which insisted upon taking seriously its right to use the veto power. In the first place, logic denies the probability that the veto was regarded as an obstructive capability that would never be used and would therefore never interfere with the operation of collective security. It is difficult to believe that the major powers worked as hard as they did to secure acceptance of the veto provision, in the conviction that it would be superfluous; this grant of a special power to a dissenter reflects the assumption that there will be dissent, not that there will be unity. The veto provision was not inserted in the Charter in a fit of absentmindedness. It was adopted with full awareness, and deliberate intent, that any of the major powers might use it to block collective action. Its insertion can only be interpreted as a declaration that the United Nations should not and could not be drawn into any attempt to implement the principle of collective security in opposition to a great power.[9]

[9] For an early and perceptive statement of this interpretation see Wellington Koo, Jr., *Voting Procedures in International Political Organizations* (New York: Columbia, 1947), pp. 117, 124, 134.

We need not rely solely upon logical analysis of the provisions of the Charter for evidence that the original United Nations scheme involved a repudiation of the ambition to construct a collective security system which would be operative in the type of case most critically relevant to the issue of global war or peace. The records of the San Francisco Conference show that the participants were thoroughly aware of the fact that, in adopting the veto provision, they were renouncing that ambition. The United States declared that the veto rule "meant that if a major power became the aggressor the Council had no power to prevent war." [10] An Indian spokesman warned against the delusion "that the proposed Organization could prevent wars between the great nations or even between small nations, if the great powers were divided in their sympathies." [11] The general understanding of the import of the veto rule was expressed by a delegate from New Zealand, who said that it made collective security impossible.[12] This interpretation of the limits of the system contemplated in the Charter was stated explicitly by Secretary of State Stettinius in the hearings on the Charter.[13]

As I have intimated, a case can be made for the proposition that the founding fathers of the United Nations engaged in some misrepresentation of their product; they did not *always* qualify their praise of the projected Organization with explicit acknowledgment of its deliberately contrived incapacity to function as a collective security agency in cases involving great-power aggression or great-power support of aggressors. Realistically, one should not have expected that they would stress this important limitation of the new Organization. We have, after all, a working understanding that statesmen are not expected or required, any more than advertisers of soap or cigarettes, to put their worst feet forward. However, the accusation that the United Nations was "oversold" by its creators and sponsors has often been made too loosely and without adequate consideration of all the evidence.[14]

The sober truth about the built-in restrictions on the capability of the United Nations as an organ of collective security was frequently and prominently stated. There is, indeed, ample evidence that this limitation was widely understood within the interested United States public.

[10] UN Information Organizations and U. S. Library of Congress, *Documents of the United Nations Conference on International Organization* (New York, 1945), XI, p. 514.

[11] *Ibid.*, XII, pp. 307–308

[12] *Ibid.*, p. 296.

[13] *The Charter of the United Nations,* Hearing Before the Committee on Foreign Relations, U. S. Senate, 79th Congress, 1st Session (Washington, 1945), p. 215.

[14] See Robert E. Riggs, "Overselling the UN Charter—Fact and Myth," *International Organization,* Spring 1960 (Vol. 14, No. 2), pp. 277–290.

The National League of Woman Voters was only one of many groups which revealed this understanding in public statements soon after the San Francisco Conference; in a memorandum inserted in the record of the hearings on the Charter, this organization stated the view that:

> If a great power becomes an aggressor, the United Nations Organization will not be able to act, and the situation will have to be handled outside the Organization. This is because we are still in the experimental stage of collective security, and world opinion has not yet developed to the point where nations are willing to delegate sufficient authority to an international organization to make it capable of coercing a great power.[15]

The Senate Committee on Foreign Relations proved itself both cognizant of and eager to encourage public understanding of the inherent limitations of the United Nations when it took care to point out, in its report on the Charter, that:

> neither this Charter nor any other document or formula that might be devised can prevent war, and the committee would be performing a disservice to the public if its action with respect to the Charter should indicate any such opinion on its part.

The committee held that the creation of the new Organization "will at best be a beginning toward the creation of those conditions of stability throughout the world which will foster peace and security." [16]

The evidence leads me to the conclusion that the formulators of the United Nations Charter deliberately refrained from attempting to create an organization which would undertake to control the use of force by great powers or states supported by them, through the operation of a collective security system. They acted on the assumption that such a venture could not succeed, and ought not to be attempted. In this fundamentally important sense, the establishment of the United Nations represented the repudiation of the idea of collective security, not an unsuccessful effort to institutionalize its application.

What then was the nature of the scheme for management of power in international relations which the Charter set forth? The answer can be found only if we emancipate ourselves from the rigidity of the categories of balance of power, collective security, and world government.

---

[15] *The Charter of the United Nations*, Hearings . . . , p. 422. For other expressions of this viewpoint, see pp. 396, 416, 531, 585, 608, 654, 661, 707.

[16] Report of the Senate Committee on Foreign Relations on the United Nations Charter, July 16, 1945, reproduced in *Review of the United Nations Charter: A Collection of Documents*, Senate Document No. 87, 83d Congress, 2d Session (Washington, 1954), p. 68.

The influence of the collective security orientation is evident in many of the provisions of the Charter. Aggression is prohibited, though left undefined; in principle, states are deprived of the legal right to use force against each other at their own discretion, in pursuit of their unilaterally defined interests and purposes. The legitimacy of resort to international violence is made subject to the determination of an international body; an effort is made even to hold states accountable to an international body in their invocation and exercise of the right of defensive action. Moreover, the principle is asserted that any illegitimate use of force in international relations is properly a matter of concern to all Members of the United Nations. The Security Council is expected to be equipped, through agreements to be concluded with Member States, with military forces constantly ready for action at its decision; it bears the responsibility for taking action to uphold peace and security and has a general authority to command the assistance of all member states—except that their obligation to provide military units is limited to the commitments which may be stated in their agreements with the Security Council.[17]

In its restriction of the right of states to resort to force, its espousal of the principle of collective action to repress illegal violence, and its provision for an organ to preside over the arrangements pertaining to the use of force, the UN scheme exhibits some of the essential characteristics of a collective security system. It should be noted that it is incomplete, in that the acceptance by states of an operative obligation to put force at the disposal of the Security Council—and, consequently, the equipping of the Council to perform its enforcement role—is postponed; on this score, the Charter registers merely an agreement to agree. Nevertheless, the scheme clearly reflects the intention to create an international enforcement mechanism capable of functioning in cases which do not involve a conflict of interest and will among the great powers. It might be described as a design for a collective security system applicable only to situations of relatively minor importance as far as maintenance of the general peace is concerned. The framers of the Charter contemplated a system in which the great powers would bear the major responsibility for providing United Nations enforcement potential, with supplementary contributions by lesser states, for the purpose of dealing with aggressors acting without the support or sympathy of any of the major powers. The great powers, it should be recalled, persistently spoke at San Francisco of the "unanimity rule,"

[17] This summary of the scheme is based upon Articles 2, 24–25, and 39–51 of the Charter.

not the "veto rule," thereby emphasizing the positive hope that the Security Council would be able to act decisively against aggression insofar as its permanent members could achieve unanimity in supporting such action. There was no middle ground in this arrangement. Either an act of aggression would be committed by a minor state with all the major powers ranged against it, in which case collective suppression of the misdeed would be a relatively simple matter, or it would be committed by a major power or its protégé, in which case the United Nations would be debarred from attempting collective suppression. Although the applicability of the United Nations enforcement scheme to the control of the defeated Axis powers of World War II was excluded, it was provided that this limitation might be removed at the request of the victorious allies.[18]

The key prescription of the Charter for dealing with the potential crises of greatest international importance—those involving antagonism among the great powers or aggressive action undertaken or sponsored by one or more of the great powers—is to be found in Article 51, with its recognition of "the inherent right of individual or collective self-defense" in response to armed attack. This provision may be interpreted as a declaration that it is incumbent upon states to take the necessary measures, outside the structure of the United Nations, for dealing with the most crucial threats to peace and security which might arise. The framers of the Charter were saying, in effect, that they saw no possibility of implementing collective security safely and effectively against major powers, and that some device other than collective security would have to be improvised if a major power should go on the warpath. They did not, as has often been suggested, assume that no such problem would arise; in this respect, they were hopeful but not smugly confident. Rather, they asserted the conviction that it was impossible to construct a collective security system adequate to deal with such a problem, if it should arise. The advice implicit in Article 51 is that states should establish alliances—combinations for collective self-defense—for dealing with the actuality or threat of attack by powers exempted by the veto rule from the impact of the projected United Nations enforcement mechanism.

In this vitally important respect, the Charter contemplates what is in essence a balance of power system. This was no doubt an unhappy choice for the founding fathers. Their ideological bias clearly ran not toward the balance of power but toward collective security. Their sense of realism, however, impelled them to acknowledge that they could

[18] See Articles 53 and 107 of the Charter.

see no way to devise a workable alternative to the balance of power system for dealing with aggressive threats posed directly or indirectly by great powers. It should be noted that the balance of power system, involving the freedom and responsibility of states to look to their own position within the international configuration of power, does not have to be adopted; it exists, until and unless an alternative arrangement for managing the power relationships of states is put into effect. Failing even to formulate—much less to put into effect—a more centralized scheme for handling conflicts in which major powers might be competitively engaged, the creators of the United Nations left states to "do what comes naturally" in such situations: that is, to develop the power and policy, individually and in alignment with others, for coping with security threats presented by dangerously powerful antagonists.

The original scheme of the United Nations for the management of power on the international scene may thus be described as one which left the balance of power system intact for cases of major importance to global peace and order, and provided for a collective security system to be applicable in cases of relatively minor significance. The Charter endorsed the *ideal* of collective security in unqualified terms, but envisaged its application in severely limited terms. It limited the legal right of states, great or small, to engage in the unfettered maneuvering which has been traditionally associated with the operation of a balance of power system, and reflected the hope that the political processes of the United Nations would inhibit the tendency of states to abuse their strength under the pretext of protecting their relative power positions. In the final analysis, however, the Charter acknowledged that the new Organization could not relieve states of the necessity of attempting on their own to match power with power, as the means of attaining security within the context of great-power rivalry. The scheme of the Charter was a curious amalgam of collective security, dominant in ideological terms, and balance of power, dominant in terms of practical application. The concept of world government, insofar as it figured at all in the consideration of the San Francisco Conference, was viewed as a distant ideal.

II

The history of the actual operation of the United Nations in the realm of power politics is largely a story of vacillation concerning the degree to which the implementation of collective security should be attempted, and of efforts to find other means by which international organization can be used to modify the working of a balance of power system. The reluctance with which the framers of the Charter viewed the continued dependence of the world, by default, upon the balance of power system has been shared by many of the statesmen who have shaped the subsequent development of the United Nations.

One of the first tasks which confronted the new Organization was that of attempting to create the enforcement mechanism envisaged in Chapter VII—and particularly in Articles 43 and 45—of the Charter. This project, essential to the fulfillment of the promise that the Security Council would function as an agent of collective security in cases not involving discord among the major powers, was fundamentally dependent upon the capacity of the Big Five to agree concerning their contributions to the military force the Council would have at its disposal. Those powers undertook, within the Military Staff Committee and the Security Council, to reach agreement; they failed in 1947, and, despite occasional expressions of interest in trying again, they have not seriously reopened the issue since that time.

These abortive negotiations were marked by a curious refusal on the part of the United States to recognize and adhere to the principle that the United Nations enforcement system was to be operative only against minor aggressors which neither possessed the veto power nor enjoyed the protection of a great power's capacity to block Security Council action. This deviation from the understanding reached at San Francisco was implicitly expressed in a United States position which insisted that a relatively large force should be assigned to the Security Council; the other powers, estimating the requirements of the Council more modestly,[19] evidently based their proposals on the assumption that the force was intended to be used, and therefore needed to be strong enough for effective use, only in coercing states of minor military importance. The United States' deviation was stated explicitly in the argument that the Council should be equipped "to bring to bear, against any breach of the peace anywhere in the world, balanced striking forces drawn from the most powerful and best equipped forces that could be provided by the Members," so that the organization could "enforce peace in all parts of the world."[20] It appeared that the United States had either forgotten or repudiated the consensus, registered in the veto provision of the Charter, that the United Nations should not be constitutionally capable of functioning as an instrument

[19] For the provisional estimates submitted by the five permanent members of the Security Council, see *Yearbook of the United Nations, 1947–1948,* p. 495.

[20] Security Council *Official Records,* 138th Meeting, June 4, 1947, pp. 954–955, 956.

of collective security against, or in opposition to the will of, any of the major powers.

If the United States confused the negotiations with the claim that the task was to create a universally applicable system of collective security, the real lesson of the negotiations was that neither the Soviet Union nor the West seemed sufficiently trustful of the other to contemplate joint action under United Nations auspices for implementing collective security even in a limited range of cases. The various items of disagreement which plagued the discussions all pointed to the same conclusion: each of the major contestants, the Soviet Union and the United States, feared that the other might attempt to dominate any collective action in which it participated, using the pretext of serving the United Nations as a means of exploiting troubled situations to its own ends.[21] One or the other of the great powers may, of course, have been actuated by ulterior motives. What appears from the record of negotiations, however, is that this mutual suspicion operated to force the discarding of the scheme for establishing a limited collective security system under the United Nations. Collective security operations pitting great powers against each other had been excluded in the original design; collective security operations involving collaboration among the great powers were now seen to be politically infeasible.

This initial decline to zero of the modest expectations of collective security entertained by the drafters of the Charter was sharply reversed by the events of 1950. The United Nations response to North Korean aggression against South Korea was attributable to a unique complex of circumstances, and it was not by any means a "pure" example of collective security in action. Nevertheless, the early phase of the collective military action in Korea under the banner of the United Nations produced among its participants and supporters an exhilarating sense of involvement in an unprecedented effort to give effect to the principle of collective security. Member States found themselves joined together to suppress an act of aggression which could plausibly be regarded as one sponsored or supported by two major powers, the Soviet Union and Communist China, and they seemed likely to carry off this bold enterprise both successfully and safely. They had, by improvising a reasonable facsimile of collective security action to meet North Korean aggression, cast aside what now seemed the excessive timidity of the framers of the Charter, who had believed it would be

[21] See my analysis of this point in "The United Nations and the Use of Force," *International Conciliation*, March 1961. Cf. William Reitzel, Morton A. Kaplan, and Constance G. Coblenz, *United States Foreign Policy, 1945–1955* (Washington: Brookings Institution, 1956), pp. 239–240.

neither possible nor prudent for the United Nations to take action in such cases.

The sudden enthusiasm for collective security engendered by the Korean action was translated into support for the Uniting for Peace Resolution, a United States initiative adopted by the General Assembly in the fall of 1950.[22] This scheme involved an assertion by the General Assembly of competence to take over the consideration of threatening situations from a veto-bound Security Council, designate the aggressor, and recommend collective action by Member States. Among other things, it provided for the establishment of a Collective Measures Committee to study the problems of giving effect to the principle of collective security, and called upon states to designate special military units for possible participation in future United Nations enforcement actions. Concretely, this was a plan for enabling the United Nations to react in future situations as it had in Korea. While the Uniting for Peace plan fell short of a full-fledged collective security system, notably in its failure to provide for obligatory participation by states in sanctions, it was clearly put forward as a device for transforming the United Nations into an agency of universal collective security.[23]

Thus, the United Nations moved in 1950 from the expectation that no collective security action would be forthcoming in any case, to the hypothetical possibility of collective security action in every case of aggression. In adopting the Uniting for Peace plan, Members of the United Nations purported to express the determination to develop an international enforcement system applicable even to violations of the peace in which great powers might be directly or indirectly involved. In scope, if not in legal depth, this plan for collective security was far more ambitious than that stated in the Charter.

This was the high-water mark of enthusiasm for turning the United Nations into a collective security system. The flood receded rather quickly and, apparently, irreversibly. The later stages of the Korean conflict engendered second thoughts about the desirability of repeating that experiment. By the time Members of the United Nations had managed to disengage themselves from active fighting in Korea, they had developed a renewed appreciation for the prudence of the founding fathers who had decreed that the Organization ought not to attempt collective action in the face of great-power opposition. Uncommitted states came gradually to recognize that they had a stake in preventing

[22] General Assembly Resolution 377 (V), November 3, 1950.
[23] See General Assembly *Official Records,* Fifth Session, 295th Plenary Meeting, October 24, 1950, p. 246, and 299th Plenary Meeting, November 1, 1950, pp. 291–292.

the United Nations from being invoked as an instrumentality of one
side against the other in "cold war" conflicts; in these terms, the veto
was not so much a special privilege of the great powers as a protection
for the minor powers against being pulled, through their membership
in the United Nations, into the maelstrom of great-power struggle. The
United States, which had conceived the Uniting for Peace plan as a
device primarily for legitimizing and mobilizing support for Western
action in resistance to Soviet expansionism, gradually lost confidence
that the General Assembly could be counted on to put the plan to that
use, and began to doubt both the wisdom and the utility of the venture
in enhancing the quasi-collective security possibilities of the United
Nations which it had sponsored.

The earliest indication of the subsiding of collective security sentiment was provided by the hesitation of Member States to respond
positively to the suggestion they had addressed to themselves in the
Uniting for Peace Resolution, *i.e.*, that they set aside definite military.
units for possible use in United Nations enforcement actions. This
recommendation produced little more than vague affirmations that
armed forces might under certain circumstances be supplied; in effect,
this project for developing a military arm of the United Nations was
soon relegated to the dead-letter office along with Article 43, which it had
been intended to replace.

The Hungarian and Suez crises of 1956 produced further evidence
that the aspirations for giving effect to collective security, so fervently
expressed in 1950, had been dispelled by sober second thoughts. In
these critical cases, both involving coercive action by great powers, the
Uniting for Peace plan was invoked and was operative to the point
of bringing about condemnation by the General Assembly of the Soviet
Union in the one case, and of the United Kingdom, France, and Israel
in the other. The latter three states, involved in attacks upon Egypt,
were induced to withdraw and thus to spare the Assembly the necessity of deciding whether it should attempt to organize collective compulsion. The Soviet Union, having ruthlessly suppressed the Hungarian
Revolution, stood in defiance of an Assembly which gave no evidence
of even considering the possibility of attempting to impose military
sanctions.

The position of the United States in these two cases reveals the
extent to which the urge for collective security had declined since the
adoption of the Uniting for Peace Resolution. In the Suez case, the
United States exhibited a measure of devotion to the collective security
ideology in supporting the condemnation of friends and allies for their

attack upon a state whose behavior the United States patently disapproved. United States leaders, however, clearly had no stomach for
the possibility of being called upon to participate in coercive measures
to enforce the Assembly's demands against the United Kingdom,
France, and Israel. Most notably, they were appalled at the thought
that the Soviet Union might use "participation in collective security
action under the United Nations" as a device for establishing a foot-
hold in the Middle East. When President Eisenhower recoiled at the
"unthinkable" suggestion of the Soviet Union that the two giant powers
join to enforce the will of the United Nations in that region,[24] he was
giving new expression to the mistrust which had been apparent in
the negotiations, in 1947, for creating a United Nations force to be
placed at the disposal of the Security Council. The notion of a collective
security action which would bring Soviet Union forces into the
Middle East was profoundly unattractive to the United States.

In the Hungarian case, the United States demonstrated that it was
equally unattracted by the idea of leading or participating in collective
action against the Soviet Union, lest such a move precipitate a general
war. In refraining from the initiation of a collective campaign to oust
Soviet Union forces from Hungary, the Assembly was supporting, not
frustrating, the policy of the United States. This was the sort of case
for which the Uniting for Peace plan had ostensibly been designed;
the fact that collective measures against the Soviet Union were not
seriously contemplated was evidence that the ambition to overcome the
veto barrier to the functioning of the United Nations as an agency
of collective security had been abandoned.

We have seen that the history of the United Nations has been
marked by the fluctuation of sentiment regarding the desirability and
feasibility of making the Organization a mechanism to implement the
principle of collective security. It seems likely that the ephemeral
enthusiasm for collective security engendered by the early phase of
the Korean experience and registered in the Uniting for Peace Resolution will prove the last flurry for some time to come. The creators of
the United Nations envisaged an extremely modest version of collective
security; in the present situation, there is no evidence that Members of
the Organization entertain either the expectation or the intention of
operating a collective security system, limited or universal in its impact,
within the institutional framework of the United Nations. Force may
be used for limited purposes under United Nations auspices in particular cases, as in the Congo, for instance. This, however, does not imply
that there is a meaningful possibility of organizing a dependable system

[24] *New York Times,* November 6, 1956, p. 10.

of collective military sanctions to repel international aggression. The repudiation of the urge to establish collective security as an operative system for the management of power in international relations appears, for the foreseeable future, definitive.

The Charter's implicit recognition of the necessity for a residual balance of power system to cope with great-power antagonisms has had substantially greater effect than its design for a collective security system to deal with situations of less critical importance. Once it became clear that a struggle between the Soviet Union and the West was to be the dominant motif of postwar international relations, the process of alliance-building and of competitive armament began. On the Western side, the formulation of the North Atlantic Treaty represented an acknowledgment that no alternative to the methods characteristic of the balance of power system could be envisaged for meeting the threat of Soviet Union aggressiveness. It is notable that the United States responded to the lesson of communist aggression in Korea, not simply by sponsoring the Uniting for Peace plan, but also by taking the lead in strengthening the Western alliance, both militarily and institutionally, giving it the form of the North Atlantic Treaty Organization. In the one case, the United States endorsed the ideology of collective security; in the other, it expressed the intent to seek security within the context of a balance of power system. There can be little doubt that the latter was the more significant move, the more reliable indicator of the emphasis which was to characterize United States foreign policy. While the doctrine of collective security has been alternately played up and played down in the United Nations, statesmen have treated the problem of maneuvering successfully within the framework of a balance of power system as the serious business of contemporary diplomacy. This represents the confirmation, not the invalidation, of the assumption expressed in the Charter; if one considers the combination of Articles 27 and 51 of the Charter, one finds the statesmen of San Francisco implying that security problems stemming from discord among the giants call for the application of the concept of balance of power, not the concept of collective security. Great-power antagonisms have dominated the international scene, and they have evoked the type of response which the Charter indicated would be necessary.

In the final analysis, then, the effort to control the use of force in international relations since World War II has been expressed in the form of a balance of power system. What has emerged is a balance system modified by a number of factors including, most significantly for purposes of this analysis, the existence of a general international organization. It would be too much to say that the United Nations "presides over" the operation of the balance of power system, but its functioning does have considerable relevance to the working of that system.

The real question for our time is not whether the United Nations is likely to develop a collective security system—or, more remotely, to institute a scheme for the management of power which would deserve the name of world government—to replace the balance of power system. The real question relates to the manner in which, and the degree to which, the United Nations can and will modify the operation of the balance system and contribute to its success as a device for preventing war. In facilitating diplomatic confrontation, fostering serious and meaningful negotiation, and providing assistance in the pacific settlement of disputes, the Organization plays a role which may be useful in mitigating the dangers of failure. In putting moral and political pressure upon states to conform to the principles of international conduct which the Charter prescribes, the United Nations may help to limit the abusive aspects of state behavior which balance of power operations may otherwise entail. In carrying out its wide-ranging activities within the economic and social sectors, the Organization may contribute to a long-term transformation of the global situation which will create new possibilities for the effective management of the power problem.

Finally, it should be noted that a role for the United Nations, more immediately and directly related to the issue of military violence, has been for some time in the process of development. In a number of instances, the Organization has secured and provided military personnel for supervising truce arrangements, patrolling armistice lines, observing developments in zones of particular instability, and otherwise contributing to the maintenance of precariously peaceful relationships. Against this background, an act of creative political ingenuity occurred in 1956, when the Organization was given the mission of mobilizing a United Nations Emergency Force, composed exclusively of military elements from states other than great powers, to function as a stabilizer of the dangerously tense situation in the Middle East. When a somewhat analogous, albeit infinitely more complex, situation arose in the Congo in 1960, the machinery of the United Nations was again used to organize and carry out a military operation.

There were basic differences in the tasks required of United Nations forces in these two situations. What is important for this analysis, however, is the element of similarity in the two cases. In both instances, the United Nations was used as a device for bringing into a troubled situation military contingents contributed voluntarily by smaller states and placed under the direction of the Secretary-General, for the purpose of preventing the eruption of disorders that might result in the competitive intervention of the rival great-power blocs. This is a far cry from the original notion of a United Nations enforcement system which would depend upon the unanimous participation of the great powers; it expresses the notion of a United Nations stabilization system dependent upon the unanimous abstention of the great powers.[25] Such a system cannot be forced upon unwilling great powers. It can function successfully only with their acquiescence, derived from the recognition that they have a stake in the avoidance of conflicts that might precipitate war. Intervention by the United Nations in the Middle East and in the Congo represents the experimental development of a significant role for the Organization in the balance of power system, that of assisting in its orderly operation by undertaking to insulate particular trouble-spots from the impact of the rivalry which dominates the relationships of the major powers. This experimentation, whatever its outcome, is a hopeful sign, for it points to the general recognition of a basic truth: *i.e.*, that the potential contribution of the United Nations in our time to the management of international power relationships lies not in implementing collective security or instituting world government, but in helping to improve and stabilize the working of the balance of power system which is, for better or for worse, the operative mechanism of contemporary international politics.

MILITARY POWER AND INTERNATIONAL ORDER [*] [1]

Michael Howard

Michael Howard is Professor of War Studies in the University of London and a military historian who also comments on contemporary

[25] Cf. Lincoln P. Bloomfield, *The United Nations and U. S. Foreign Policy* (Boston: Little, Brown, 1960), pp. 44–45, 67.

[*] From Michael Howard, "Military Power and International Order," *International Affairs*, 40, No. 3 (July 1964), pp. 397–408. Reprinted by permission of Michael Howard.
[1] This is a slightly abridged version of Professor Howard's inaugural lecture delivered at King's College, London, on May 5, 1964.

military affairs. His chief historical work is a definitive history of the Franco-Prussian War.

In his inaugural lecture, in January 1927, my predecessor, Sir Frederick Maurice,[2] chose as his subject 'The Uses of the Study of War'. These uses he saw as twofold.

The first, which most concerns the citizen, is to promote peace by promoting an understanding of the realities of war and of the problems which may lead to war. The second, which most concerns the professional, but also does or should concern the citizen, is to ensure that war, if it comes, is waged in the best possible way.

For, he pointed out,

A struggle between nations in which vital interests are involved is not merely the concern of professional soldiers, sailors and airmen, but affects directly every citizen and calls for the whole resources of the nation. We have learned that statecraft, economics, the supply of raw material, science and industry, are factors which are of prime importance to the issue, and we realise that the tendency is for the importance of the last two to increase . . .

Above all (he concluded) we have learned that war is a great evil.

The course of the Second World War was to bear out everything that he said. Its outcome was determined as much in the factories and shipyards and laboratories as on the battlefield itself. Its historians have to study the development of weapon-design and production, and problems of political, economic and industrial organisation, at least as deeply as the operations of the armed forces themselves. Yet it is quite clear that the development of weapons during the last 20 years has effected so drastic a change in the nature of war that Sir Frederick's lecture can now properly be read only as a historical document from a previous era. Only by considering the context in which it was delivered and assessing the extent and significance of the changes which have since occurred can we take his words as a guide to our own studies and policies in the second half of the 20th century.

What was this context? It was that of the age of struggles between 'Nations in Arms' which had opened with the French Revolutionary Wars, developed through those great mid-century conflicts between nascent industrial communities, the American Civil War and the Franco-Prussian War, and reached its climax in the two World Wars which dominated the first half of this century. During this period,

[2] Major-General Sir Frederick Maurice was Professor of War Studies, King's College, University of London, from 1929 to 1933.

the development of the political authority and administrative expertise of the state made it possible to place at the disposal of the armed forces the entire resources of the nation in man-power, technical skill and industrial productivity. The development of science, engineering and industry made equally available to them, in great quantities, weapons of unprecedented destructive power. Equipped with these weapons, making full use of all developing means of transport by land, sea, and, ultimately, air, and drawing on national man-power to the point of exhaustion, the armed forces of the great nations of the Northern hemisphere were able to pursue on a gigantic scale the classical objectives of warfare: the defeat of the opposing forces, in order to disarm the enemy and confront him with the alternatives of annihilation or surrender; or at least a sufficient probability of defeat to make it sound policy for him to come to terms.

As the 20th century progressed the means of achieving this objective grew even more complex and sophisticated, but the object itself remained unaltered. The hopes expressed by inter-war theorists, that direct military confrontation might be avoided or mitigated by direct assaults on the morale of the enemy population, whether by propaganda, by blockade or by air attack, bore very little fruit. Command of the air could not be won without first destroying the enemy air force in a subtle and long-drawn-out battle of attrition; and without command of the air it was not possible to strike effectively either at the enemy population or at his sources of economic strength. Without command of the sea the economic base of maritime nations was hopelessly vulnerable; and command of the sea was the reward of a weary struggle, not simply between capital fleets as Mahan and his disciples had believed, but between submarines, escorts, aircraft and surface-raiders, equipped with the finest aids science could provide but ultimately dependent on the courage and skill of the men who manned them. Armies were still needed to seize or defend the bases on which command of the air or the sea depended and to exploit the opportunities which these advantages gave them; and even without these advantages skilful leadership, good weapons and stubborn troops could still inflict heavy losses and impose heartbreaking delays.

For all these reasons, and in spite of the growing complication of war in three elements, one can still trace in the Second World War the basic characteristics of the conflicts waged by Napoleon, by Ulysses S. Grant, by Moltke, and by Ludendorff and Haig. There was the mobilisation of the resources of the nation, involving a transformation of the peacetime pattern of the national economy. There was the conversion of those resources into effective military power; and there was the deployment of that power by military specialists, according to classical principles of strategy, for the defeat of the enemy armed forces.

It is of course an over-simplification to talk of the age of mass-warfare as 'beginning' in 1792. Eighteenth-century habits of military thought and organisation lingered long into the 19th and even the 20th centuries—perhaps longer in this sheltered country than anywhere else. Very few of Goethe's contemporaries could have understood what he meant by observing that a new age had opened when the French volunteers stood firm under the Prussian cannonade at Valmy on September 20, 1792. But there was no lack of would-be Goethes to proclaim the beginning of a new era on August 6, 1945, when the first atomic bomb was dropped on Hiroshima. In the short run they were wrong, just as Goethe was wrong. The atom bombs of 1945, for all their unprecedented power, were not immediately accepted by military planners as being, in themselves, decisive weapons of war. Their process of manufacture was so slow and expensive that it was several years before the United States had a stockpile sufficient to devastate a rival as large as the Soviet Union; while such bombs as were available could be transported to their targets only in sub-sonic, short-range manned bombers, vulnerable to fighter attack and anti-aircraft fire. When the world began to rearm again in 1950 the atom bomb was considered an ancillary and not a decisive weapon in a conflict which, in the view of responsible defence specialists on both sides, was likely to differ little in its basic requirements from the Second World War. The year 1945, like 1792, only provided a foretaste of what might come when the new technology got into its stride; that is, when thermonuclear replaced atomic explosives, and manned bombers were supplemented by ballistic missiles.

It is tempting to draw from this development sweeping and premature conclusions. There are still very few nuclear Powers in the world, and it seems unlikely that their number will increase very rapidly. A conflict today between, say, China and India, or between two African states, might well conform to the general pattern of European warfare over the past hundred years. But for the great industrial nations of the Northern hemisphere, that pattern is now radically altered. In order to confront one's adversary with the alternatives of annihilation or surrender it is no longer necessary to mobilise major forces and deploy them according to classical principles of strategy. It is unlikely that there will be either the need or the time to apply the techniques we learned in two world wars for the switching over of the national economy from a peacetime to a wartime footing. Those Powers which possess sufficient wealth, scientific expertise and industrial capacity have developed weapons-systems which poise the threat of inescapable and unacceptable destruction over the heads of their rivals even in time of deepest peace; and for nations so threatened military security can no longer be based on traditional principles of defence, mobilisation and counter-attack. It can be based only on the capacity to deter one's adversary by having available the capacity to inflict on him inescapable and unacceptable damage in return.

So much has been generally accepted for the past 10 years, and the dimensions of this new situation have been studied with encyclopaedic brilliance by a group of American scholars whose work must be the starting point for any student of military affairs today. They have patiently unravelled the problems of the technical and political requirements of deterrence. They have discussed the possible nature of a nuclear war, the alternative forms into which international conflict might be channelled, and the political measures needed to control the military forces we can now unleash. But many things remain unclear: not least of them the effect which this transformation in the nature of war is likely to have on that international order in which armed sovereign states peacefully coexist; always assuming that they remain armed and that they remain sovereign—two assumptions which at present it seems not unreasonable to make.

* * *

In offering some tentative remarks on this subject I shall consider briefly the nature both of war and of the international order within which it arises. I shall not, in dealing with the first, adopt the view that war is a disease of the body politic, a pathological condition which can be traced to abnormalities in the social or economic structure, or to the racial characteristics of particular peoples. One could list many such explanations of the causes of war, from 'aggressor nations' or the machinations of armament-manufacturers to particular kinds of ruling class—whether monarcho-feudal, as the Cobdenites believed 100 years ago, or bourgeois-capitalist, as the socialists believed 50 years later. All take as their starting point the assumption that peace is the natural condition of mankind, as health is of the human body. Such a view is understandable enough. It is a commendable reaction, not simply against the evils of war in themselves, but against the doctrines which were so widespread in Europe during the 19th and the earlier part of this century, that War is necessary to the health of the Race, that it is an intrinsic part of the dialectical mechanism of Progress or the biological mechanism of the Survival of the Fittest, a test of manhood to be strenuously prepared for and welcomed when it comes. The generation of Rupert Brooke had still to learn the lesson, on which Sir Frederick Maurice was to insist in 1927, that 'war is a great evil'.

But the.historian and the political scientist cannot discuss war in terms of good or evil, normality or abnormality, health or disease. For them it is simply the use of violence by states for the enforcement, the protection or the extension of their political power. Some wars, under some circumstances, may be rational acts of policy; under others, they may not. Power, in itself, is something morally neutral, being no more than the capacity of individuals or groups to control and organise their environment to conform with their physical requirements or their code of moral values. The desire for, acquisition, and exercise of power is the raw material of politics, national and international, and violence may sometimes prove an effective means to secure or retain it. Within well-organised states groups can seldom achieve power by violence, save in a marginal or covert way; and power which is so achieved will be of a most transitory kind until it is transformed by prescriptive exercise or rational consent into effective authority. Yet in spite of the aspirations of internationalists since the 16th century, in spite of Hague Conferences, Kellogg Pacts, League Covenants and United Nations Charters, the use of violence remains among sovereign states as an accepted if rarely exercised instrument for the extension or protection of their power.

But the inhibitions on the use of violence between states are considerable. They are not grounded simply on humanitarian considerations, or on any formal respect for international law. Fundamentally they rest on the most naked kind of self-interest. The use of violence, between states as between individuals, is seldom the most effective way of settling disputes. It is expensive in its methods and unpredictable in its outcome; and these elements of expense and unpredictability have both grown enormously over the last 100 years. The advent of nuclear weapons has only intensified an aversion to the use of violence in international affairs, which has, with certain rather obvious exceptions, increasingly characterised the conduct of foreign policy by the major Powers since the latter part of the 19th century.

For this aversion there was little historical precedent. In most of the societies known to history, war has been an established and usually rather enjoyable social rite. In Western Europe until the first part of the 17th century warfare was a way of life for considerable sections of society, its termination was for them a catastrophe, and its prolongation, official or unofficial, was the legitimate objective of every man of spirit. Even in the 17th and 18th centuries war, elaborate and formal as its conduct had become, was an accepted, almost an indispensable part of the pattern of society, and it was curtailed and intermittent only because of its mounting expense. If war could be made to pay, as it did for the Dutch merchants in the 17th century and the English in the 18th, then its declaration was as welcome as its termination was deplored. Habits of mind formed in days when war was the main social function of the nobility and a source of profit to the merchants survived into our own century, even though new weapons had rendered aristocratic leadership anachronistic if not positively dangerous, and the City of London confidently predicted ruin and bankruptcy when war threatened in 1914. Such atavistic belligerence was fanned by the jingoistic enthusiasm of the masses in the great cities of Western Europe, where gusts of emotion greeted every war from the Crimea to that of 1914.

But by 1914 governments and peoples were largely at cross-purposes. Since 1870 the size and expense of the war-machines, and the uncertainty of the consequences of war for society as a whole, made violence an increasingly unusable instrument for the conduct of international affairs. Defeat, even at the hands of a moderate and restrained adversary, might mean social revolution, as it nearly had for France in 1870 and Russia in 1905; while even a successful war involved a disturbance of the economic life of the nation whose consequences were quite unforeseeable. Clausewitz in his great work *On War* had suggested that 'policy', the adaptation of military means to political objectives, could convert the heavy battlesword of war into a light, handy rapier for use in limited conflicts; but the mass armies of 1870, of 1914 and of 1939 could not be wielded as rapiers in the cut and thrust of international politics. Indeed, so great was the expense of modern war, so heavy were the sacrifices that it entailed, that it was difficult to conceive of causes warranting having resort to it at all. Could the national resources really be mobilised and the youth of the nation really be sacrificed in hundreds of thousands for anything short of national survival, or some great ideological crusade?

So at least it appeared to the great Western democracies in the 1930s; and it was this sentiment that Hitler exploited with such superb and sinister skill. Mass war, as Britain and France had learned to fight it between 1914 and 1918, was not a rational instrument of foreign policy. French and British statesmen were naturally and properly unwilling to invoke it for such limited objectives as the preservation of the Rhineland from re-militarisation; or the prevention of the *Anschluss* of an acquiscent Austria with Germany; or to prevent the German population of the Sudetenland being accorded the privileges of self-determination which had been granted to other peoples in Central Europe; and there appeared to be no other instruments they could use instead. To suggest that Hitler could not have been planning for war because in 1939 the German economy was not fully mobilised nor the armed forces at full battle strength is to apply the standards of 1914 to a different situation. Hitler had not armed Germany, as Britain and France had systematically armed since 1935, for a full-scale, formal Armageddon. He had every hope that it might be avoided. But he had the means available to use violence as an instrument of policy in a limited but sufficient degree, and he had no more inhibitions about using it in foreign than he had in domestic affairs. The Western democracies, committed to a policy of total violence in international affairs or none at all, could only watch him paralysed; until they took up arms on a scale, and with a crusading purpose, which could result only in the destruction of Germany or of themselves, and quite conceivably of both.

We should not, therefore, overestimate the change brought about in international relations through the introduction of nuclear weapons. The reluctance to contemplate the use of such weapons, which is fortunately so characteristic of the Powers which at present possess them, is a continuation, although vastly intensified, of the reluctance to use the older techniques of mass war. Even as the statesmen of the 1930s found it difficult to conceive of a cause urgent enough to justify the use of the massive weapons of which they potentially disposed, so, *a fortiori*, is it still more difficult for us to foresee the political problem to which the destruction of a score of millions of civilians will provide the appropriate military solution. It is for this reason that political influence does not necessarily increase in direct proportion to the acquisition of nuclear power. Similarly, there is no cause to suppose that the capacity to use nuclear weapons will be any more effective as a deterrent to, or even as an agent of, disturbances of the international order than was, in the 1930s, the ability, given the will, to wage mass war. Those who wish to use violence as an instrument of policy—and since 1945 they have not been rare—can find, as did Hitler, more limited and effective forms; and those who hope to counter it need equally effective instruments for doing so.

Perhaps indeed, it is necessary, in reassessing the place of military force in international affairs, to rid ourselves of the idea that if such force is employed it must necessarily be in a distinct 'war', formally declared, ending in a clear decision embodied in a peace treaty, taking place within a precise interval of time during which diplomatic relations between the belligerents are suspended and military operations proceed according to their own peculiar laws. We reveal the influence of this concept whenever we talk about 'the next war', or 'if war breaks out' or 'the need to deter war'. If an inescapable *casus belli* were to occur between nuclear Powers, there *might* follow a spasm of mutual destruction which the survivors, such as they were, would be justified in remembering as the Third World War; but such an outcome is by no means inevitable, and appears to be decreasingly likely. It seems more probable that a *casus belli* would provoke threats and, if necessary, execution of limited acts of violence, probably though not necessarily localised, probably though not necessarily non-nuclear; all accompanied by an intensification rather than a cessation of diplomatic intercourse. Instead of a formal state of war in which diplomacy was subordinated to the requirements of strategy, specific military operations might be carried out under the most rigorous political control. It will certainly no longer be enough for the statesman to be given general guidance to a military machine which then proceeds according to its own laws. Politics must now interpenetrate military activity at every level as thoroughly as the nervous system penetrates the tissues of a human body, carrying to the smallest muscle the dictates of a controlling will. The demands on the military for discipline and self-sacrifice will be great beyond all precedent, and the opportunities for traditional honour and glory negligible. Regiments will bear as their battle honours the names, not of the battles they have fought, but those that they have averted.

The maintenance of armed forces for this role creates many problems. Such conflicts must be waged with forces in being, and the task for which they are recruited is a thankless one. The standard of technical expertise, already high, may become still more exacting; military commanders will need exceptional political wisdom as well as military skill; but they must refrain from attempting to shape the political world to their military image, as the French Army tried to do, so tragically, in Algeria. Indeed, the tendency which has been so general during the past 15 years of regarding all international relations as an extension of warfare, and the description of national policy in such terms as 'national strategy' or 'Cold War', betrays a dangerous confusion of categories and a fundamental misunderstanding of the nature of international affairs, even in an age of bitter ideological conflict.

On the other hand, statesmen now require a deeper understanding of military matters, of the needs and capabilities and limitations of armed forces, than they have ever needed in the past. Only if there is complete mutual understanding and co-operation between civil and military leaders, only if there is effective functioning of the mechanism of command and control, only if there is entire discipline and obedience in every rank of military hierarchy can military power serve as an instrument of international order at all, rather than one of international anarchy and world destruction.

*   *   *

The order which exists between sovereign states is very different in kind from that which they maintain within their borders, but it is an order none the less, though precarious in places and everywhere incomplete. There does exist a comity of nations, an international community transcending ideological and other rivalries. Its activities in many fields —those of commerce and communications, of health and diplomatic representation, of use of the high seas and of the air—are regulated by effective and precise provisions of international law, which are for the most part meticulously observed. But even in those aspects of international relations which international law does not regulate, order still obtains. It is preserved by certain conventions of behaviour established and adjusted by a continuing and subtle process of communication and negotiations, with which not even the most revolutionary of states —neither the United States in the 18th century nor the Soviet Union in the 20th—has ever found it possible to dispense for very long. This order is based on no system of positive law, nor of natural justice, nor of clearly defined rights, nor even of agreed values. It has never been very easy for sovereign states to agree about such things. Even if the differing pattern of their international development does not lead them to adopt divergent and conflicting ideologies, states are bound by their very nature to regard the maintenance of their own power as the main criterion of all their actions and to pursue that, whatever their noble professions to the contrary. International order is based rather on recognition of disagreement, and of the limitation on one's own capacity to secure agreement. It is based on the understanding by nations that their capacity to impose and extend their own favoured order is limited by the will and effective ability of other states to impose theirs. The conduct of international relations must therefore always be a delicate adjustment of power to power, a mutual exploration of intentions and capabilities, so as to find and preserve an order which, though fully satisfying to nobody, is just tolerable to all.

The power which states exercise in international affairs is compounded of many attributes, economic, diplomatic, cultural and ideological as well as military. But military power, the capacity to use violence for the protection, enforcement or extension of authority, remains an instrument with which no state has yet found it possible completely to dispense. Indeed, it is not easy to see how international relations could be conducted, and international order maintained, if it were totally absent. The capacity of states to defend themselves, and their evident willingness to do so, provides the basic framework within which the business of international negotiation is carried on. That this framework should be as wide and as flexible as possible hardly needs arguing; but if no such limits existed, if it were known that there were no extremes of surrender and humiliation beyond which a state could not be pressed, the maintenance of international order would surely be, not easier, but incalculably more difficult. It is significant that nearly every one of the new states which has emerged since the Second World War has considered it necessary to create at least a token military force, even when the strategic need has been as negligible as the financial capacity to support it. Such a force is not purely symbolic. The ultimate test of national independence remains in the nuclear what it was in the prenuclear age: whether people are prepared to risk their lives in order to secure and preserve it.

The thesis that military power is an intrinsic part of the structure of international order is not one which will meet with unanimous approval. Attitudes towards the place of armed forces in international relations fall somewhere between two extremes. On the one hand is the view that armed forces constitute a purely destabilising factor on the international scene, and that their abolition would lead to greater stability among nations. The arguments in favour of such a view are familiar and formidable, for it is true that the weapons which a nation considers necessary to its own defence will always be likely to appear to its neighbours as an actual or potential threat to themselves. The military preparations carried out by the Triple and Dual Alliances in pre-war Europe were inspired almost wholly by considerations of self-defence, but they appeared to offer reciprocally an intolerable threat, to be countered only by yet more intensive armament. It is no doubt as difficult today for the Soviet Union to believe in the purely defensive intentions of the bombers and missiles which ring her territory, and whose devastating powers our political and military leaders frequently extol, as it is for us to believe that the powerful units with which the Soviet Union could strike at Western Europe will never be used for aggressive purposes. In any case the 'Balance of Terror' is never wholly stable. It is maintained only by constant effort, heavy expense and the dedicated work of military specialists. Those specialists must constantly be thinking of the worst possible case, and it is not always easy under the circumstances to retain a sense of proportion and to realise that this may be the least probable case. It is simpler to judge the political intentions of a possible adversary according to his military capabilities; but the actions, writings and speeches stemming from such a judgment are likely to engender reciprocal alarm and bellicosity on the other side. The result is likely to be one of those arms races which inevitably, we are told, end in war.

Much of this is unfortunately and undeniably true. Yet there is all too little evidence to show that military impotence in itself leads to stability and order. The examples of China in 1931, of Abyssinia in 1935, of Czechoslovakia and her allies in 1938, and of Western empires in the Far East in 1941 are not encouraging. Violence can appear a perfectly rational instrument of policy to a state which stands to gain important strategic, economic or political advantages from the domination of helpless and disorganised neighbours; and the experience of the 1930s suggests that under such circumstances only the prospect of immediate and effective counter-violence can make it appear irrational.

At the other extreme we have the belief that military power is not merely one element of national power and international order, but the basic factor; and that no cheque in international politics can be honoured unless there is a full supply of military power in the bank to meet it. But such a view is really no more tenable than its opposite. There are many reasons which deter even the most powerful and ruthless states from attacking their neighbours; not least the inherent drawbacks of violence as an instrument of policy which we have already considered. In certain areas of the world—Scandinavia for nearly 200 years, and now at last perhaps Western Europe—social bonds have been forged between nations which make their military power increasingly irrelevant; while many states—our own not least—have exercised an influence in world politics out of all proportion to their military strength. I would suggest, in passing, that the hypothesis that British power and prestige in the 19th century rested on the strength of the Royal Navy calls for considerably more detailed analysis and documentation than it has hitherto received.

The role of military power in international order is in fact as difficult to define as is the role of gold in economic transactions; and the controversies in the economic sphere parallel very closely those in the military. Those who believe in the primacy of military considerations in international affairs have their parallel in those economists who insist that a sound currency is the only basis for a healthy economy and who pursue policies of sound finance at whatever short-term cost in social distress. Those who deny the need for military power at all have much in common with the thinkers who would maintain that the gold standard is a shibboleth contrived by financiers for their own profit, and that a workable economic system, based perhaps on some form of Social Credit, if not on simple inflation, can be devised without reference to it at all.

To a large extent this economic controversy has died down, or at least is conducted rather more intelligently than it was 30 years ago. The thunderings of the orthodox have been muted since Lord Keynes showed how far governments could carry economic manipulation without incurring disaster. The arguments of the reformers sound less persuasive after 20 years of chronic balance-of-payment problems. We have learned that although man is not the slave of economic forces, neither is he their master; that he can sail closer to the wind than was ever thought possible, but must still take account of it; and that there are limits to what even the most accomplished sailor can do.

All this was learned—and is still being learned—not only through the hard experience of treasury officials and business men, but by the reasoning, study and debate of academic economists. Today all these three groups work, if not always in harmony, at least in fairly fruitful dialectic. But in the field of military affairs we are still in the pre-Keynesian era. Pronouncements about military power and disarmament are still made by public figures of apparent intelligence and considerable authority with a naive dogmatism of a kind such as one finds in virtually no other area of social studies or public affairs. The concepts and presuppositions on which defence policy are based are seldom subjected in this country to academic analysis of a really serious kind, and the suggestion that they should be is usually received in Whitehall with a certain lack of enthusiasm. But it is for the academics to show first that they have something to contribute; that academic habits and techniques really are relevant to the understanding of the part played by military power in international order. It is for us to prove that the studies which we are now developing in the fields of strategic theory and military history, in the social and economic aspects of defence questions, in the military aspects of international relations and international law, in the structure of military establishments and their political and constitutional relationship with civil society, do not represent simply a passing intellectual fashion but that they are both academically reputable and socially relevant.

A NEW EUROPE? *

Stephen R. Graubard

Stephen R. Graubard is editor of Daedalus, *the journal of the American Academy of Arts and Sciences and research associate of the Center for International Affairs, Harvard University. His publications include* British Labour and the Russian Revolution *and* Burke, Disraeli and Churchill: Politics and Perseverance.

. . . As Athens had been the school of the ancient Greek world, so Europe increasingly assumed that role in the seventeenth century for the whole world. Europeans rarely questioned the superiority of their ideas or techniques. Fontenelle, in his *Entretiens sur la Pluralité des Mondes,* wrote, rather characteristically: [1]

. . . there is a certain specific quality of mind or genius which you meet with nowhere but in Europe, or at any rate not far beyond it. It may be that it cannot, from its very nature, expand at once over an extended area, and that some decree of fate compels it to keep within a more or less restricted sphere. Be that as it may, let us make the most of it while it is ours. The great thing is, it is not confined to matters of science and arid philosophical speculation, it embraces art, and taste, and beauty, in which spheres I doubt if there is any race in the world to equal us.

Pride in Europe's unique qualities grew the more that Europeans became acquainted with the rest of the world. The philosophers of the Enlightenment were ardent propagandists for Europe; they did much to bring European achievement to the attention of a larger audience than the learned public. Could any greater praise have been accorded Europe than that which Voltaire chose to bestow in his biography of Louis XIV? He wrote: [2]

Already for a long time one could regard Christian Europe (except Russia) as a sort of great republic divided into several states, some monarchical, others of a mixed character; the former aristocratic, the latter popular, but all in harmony with each other, all having the same substratum

---

* From Stephen R. Graubard, "A New Europe?". Reprinted by permission from *Daedalus,* published by the American Academy of Arts and Sciences, Brookline, Massachusetts. Vol. 93, No. 1 (1964), "A New Europe?"

[1] Quoted in Paul Hazard, *The European Mind* (New Haven: Yale University Press, 1953), pp. 439–440.

[2] Voltaire, *The Age of Louis XIV* (London: Everyman, 1926), pp. 5–6.

of religion, although divided into various sects; all possessing the same principles of public and political law, unknown in other parts of the world. In obedience to these principles the European nations do not make their prisoners slaves, they respect their enemies' ambassadors, they agree as to the pre-eminence and rights of certain princes, such as the Emperor, kings and other lesser potentates, and, above all, they are at one on the wise policy of maintaining among themselves so far as possible an equal balance of power, ceaselessly carrying on negotiations, even in wartime, and sending each to the other ambassadors or less honourable spies, who can acquaint every court with the designs of any one of them, give in a moment the alarm to Europe, and defend the weakest from invasions which the strongest is always ready to attempt.

These words, written more than two centuries after the death of Erasmus, showed the influence of seventeenth-century theory on international relations; in the pride Voltaire felt concerning Europe's achievement, there is little to distinguish this statement from what might have been said in the time of Michelangelo. Voltaire was able to look away from national wars, religious strife, commercial rivalry, and see a single European civilization. His confidence in the vitality of that order was absolute. There was no disposition to question Europe's basic institutions or values. Voltaire, a citizen of France, was also a citizen of Europe. He thought about both, with equal solicitude, being quite incapable of separating one from the other.

When European civilization came to be threatened, as it was after 1789, it is noteworthy that the individual who made the most ardent plea for Europeans to join together to defeat the French revolutionaries was a British member of Parliament, Edmund Burke, who had made his name at Westminster in large part through his defense of the interests of individual nations and peoples—the American, the Irish, and the Indian. Burke had long insisted on the unique identities of specific communities; at the time of the American Revolution, he had said: "I was never wild enough to conceive that one method would serve for the whole; that the natives of Hindostan and those of Virginia could be ordered in the same manner." [3] After 1789, such differences seemed less important to Burke. European civilization stood in dire peril; Burke thought neither as a British M.P. nor as a man born in Ireland. Both for him were subsumed in a larger unity; the reality of Europe was never more obvious, and it was this tenet which made it possible for him to say: [4]

[3] Edmund Burke, "A Letter to the Sheriffs of the City of Bristol," *Works* (London: Henry Bohn, 1846), vol. II, p. 119.

[4] Edmund Burke, "Reflections on the Revolution in France," *ibid.*, Vol. III, p. 101.

Nothing is more certain than that our manners, our civilization, and all the good things which are connected with manners, and with civilization, have, in this European world of ours, depended for ages upon two principles; and were, indeed, the result of both combined; I mean the spirit of a gentleman, and the spirit of religion.

The question of whether others would choose to define Europe as Burke had, while historically important, is not relevant to our discussion. What makes Burke's view significant is that he chose to regard Europe as an entity, to which, quite obviously, England and Ireland belonged. It never occurred to him that in such an emergency the interests of England could be substantially different from those, for example, of Spain. This attitude made possible the formation of those coalitions which, after many years and numerous failures, finally brought Napoleon down. The statesmen who gathered at Vienna to "restore" Europe came with plans which did not provide for very substantial changes in the way that Europe had been governed. They, however, were not the only men with schemes for the restoration of peace in Europe. A glance at a more utopian project tells something about the sentiment that prevailed in less conservative circles at the time. Henri St. Simon, the noted French socialist, proposed a "new Europe" which would be governed by a supra-national state. This international body would keep the peace, while maintaining intact the consciousness of Europe's identity. St. Simon's prescription for order is revealing; he wrote, more wisely than is sometimes admitted, the following: [5]

Without external activity there can be no internal tranquillity. The surest method of maintaining peace in the confederation will be ceaselessly to direct its efforts outside of itself and to occupy it without a let-up on great internal public works. To people the globe with the European race, which is superior to all other races, to open the whole world to travel and to render it as habitable as Europe, that is the enterprise through which the European parliament should continually engage the activity of Europe and always keep up the momentum.

This opinion, given its source, cannot be facilely interpreted. It is impossible to dismiss it as an expression of conventional European nationalism; much less can it be taken as the self-satisfied view of someone whose position in Europe made him idealize that world and disparage all others. St. Simon, in his concern to create safeguards against the recurrence of war, settled on a scheme which he believed fitted the European temperament. By these devices, he imagined,

[5] Quoted in Frank E. Manuel, *The New World of Henri St. Simon* (Cambridge: Harvard University Press, 1956), p. 176.

Europe could be led to channel energies into productive enterprises which would keep her fully occupied. St. Simon did not believe this to be a utopian venture; he constructed on the basis of a well-understood European disposition to expand. He was exploiting Europe's love of adventure, but also, the readiness of her people to emigrate.[6]

Until the early nineteenth century, the emigration had been continuous though quantitatively small. After the Napoleonic Wars, however, and particularly toward the middle of the century, the numbers grew in almost geometric proportions. The United States, because it drew the greatest number of European immigrants, became the object of widespread European curiosity. The question of how the New World, peopled by citizens of Europe, compared with the Old, was of more than academic interest. Continued immigration depended in part on the impressions that were transmitted back; also, relations between the two continents, inevitably, would be influenced by opinions held by each about the other. The European traveler to America in the late eighteenth and early nineteenth centuries generally came away with the impression that the New World was not simply an extension of the Old. The settlers, while superficially following European ways, engaged in daily pursuits which had more to do with conquering a wilderness than with living in settled towns or in established agricultural communities. Even the most basic institutions in America showed the effects of contact with nature. European forms did not survive unchanged in the American environment.[7] Many who traveled to the New World returned with glowing reports of the freedom they found, and of the abundance which a largely unexplored continent gave promise of producing. Others, more skeptical of the virtues of the place, were disinclined to esteem it at the value set by the Americans themselves. All, however, accepted the Atlantic Ocean as a real barrier, recognizing that it separated two worlds obviously related but in no sense identical.

The most influential report on nineteenth-century America, at least for Europeans, was certainly that written by Alexis de Tocqueville. The interest of the work derived from the fact that it was not simply a report on America, but also a prophecy of what Europe must soon expect to become. De Tocqueville, traveling in America in the 1830's, came away with a novel interpretation of the differences between the Old World and the New. The originality of his account lay in the fact that he believed these differences would soon become less important, and that Europe would increasingly come to resemble America. The "passion

---

[6] *Ibid.*, pp. 171–179.
[7] Oscar Handlin, *The Americans* (Boston: Little, Brown, 1963), pp. 28–29.

for equality," which he believed was the most distinctive feature of American life, would also, he prophesied, soon overwhelm Europe. When it did, Europe's aristocratic forms would disappear, and with them would go the distinctive civilization that had been created over the centuries. Democratic ideas would prevail, and they would quickly destroy aristocratic ideals and practices. It was not to France, specifically, that de Tocqueville addressed his message, but to all who lived in the Old World and who remained faithful to traditional forms and beliefs. Europe could do nothing to prevent this evolution; she might, however, knowing a little more about the American scene, prepare for it.[8]

New societies are generally assumed to be moving in the direction of the old. De Tocqueville's argument implied a reversal of this order; he expected the old to become increasingly like the new. This was a prospect which many Europeans regarded with trepidation and misgiving. The European attitude to the United States was, as always, ambivalent. Uncertainty about the virtues of the American democratic experiment seemed amply justified, particularly in the middle decades of the century. The Civil War and Reconstruction period strained the confidence even of those who were prepared to think well of the United States. The American habit of caricaturing European society, making it appear servile and uncreative, did not encourage Europeans to admire their critics. How could they take seriously an opinion which so grossly distorted the European situation? The comments of a prominent Norwegian lawyer, O. M. Raeder, who traveled in the United States in the middle of the century and who had no reason to feel hostile towards the Americans, suggests how such opinion affected an intelligent European; Raeder wrote, quite candidly: [9]

That which has annoyed me most in my associations with the Americans is their prejudice against Europe, which they regard as hopelessly lost in slavery and wretchedness. Three-fourths of the people in the East and ninety-nine hundredths of the people in the West are fully convinced that the other side of the Atlantic is nothing but a heap of medieval feudal states, which, indeed, show some slight indication of reform here and there, but have not made much political progress and have not enough vitality to rise from the abyss of misery and corruption into which they have fallen as the result of centuries of ignorance and despotism; their doom is inevitable. . . . It is rather a big job to defend all Europe; and I have on various occasions declined to do so, no matter how agreeable it might be once in a

8 Alexis de Tocqueville, *Democracy in America*, 2 vol. (New York: Knopf, 1960).

9 Oscar Handlin, *This Was America* (Cambridge: Harvard University Press, 1949), pp. 218–219.

while to lay aside my little Norwegian, or even Scandinavian, patriotism and to pose as the champion of a whole continent. It does not help much to reject this constituency of 200,000,000 people, because people here do not recognize many differences among various nations; every European is responsible for the whole thing.

At a time when Europeans were becoming increasingly conscious of national difference, Americans insisted on seeing the Old World as a unity. This was a period in European history when leaders tended to concentrate on large industrial, commercial and imperial enterprises, calculated to bring credit to their several countries. Terms like "Holy Russia," "Imperial Germany," and "Republican France," were only partially descriptive; they were intended to evoke emotional responses, creating the illusion of large new national purposes suited to an age which placed great stock in such accomplishment. Nationalism in its nineteenth-century form, was both romantic and disruptive; it served to make the more conventional attachments to Europe seem anachronistic. J. P. T. Bury, the British historian, has spoken of this period as one where "antagonisms fostered by nationalism . . . made not only for wars, insurrections, and local hatreds—they accentuated or created new spiritual divisions in a nominally Christian Europe." [10] Gordon Craig has shown how these developments coincided with an increasing reluctance on Great Britain's part to involve herself in Europe's affairs. As Craig explains: "Britain's growing isolation after 1865 further weakened the possibility of collaborative action in the interests of peace, because it became increasingly clear that she was unwilling to accept the kind of responsibility and assume the kind of commitments which would restrain the continental realists." [11] It was nineteenth-century nationalism, then, that made the Channel appear an important barrier, if only because it encouraged the illusion that it was possible to be in Europe while ignoring European affairs. This view enjoyed an exceedingly short life; two wars in the twentieth century proved its inadequacy.

Meanwhile, coinciding with the rise of nationalism, though repudiating many of its parochial values, another view developed which ignored traditional definitions of Europe, but which aspired to create a utopia with universal implications. This was the socialist view. The socialists, in their emphasis on class and alienation, described a world where neither would exist, where all men would enjoy equality, and where national states would be as irrelevant as private property. Karl

[10] *The New Cambridge Modern History* (Cambridge: Cambridge University Press, 1960), p. 245.
[11] *Ibid.*, p. 272.

Marx, more than those whom he dubbed "utopian Socialists," looked away from Europe, and thought only in international terms. He regarded Europe as he regarded the bourgeois class; history had given it a purpose, which was to contribute to a process that would eventually issue in a universal society. Unwittingly, Europe, even in her imperialist ventures, was creating the mechanisms which would press the world forward into the next stage. Marx's views on Great Britain's role in India are instructive; they are without sentimentality, either about one or about the other. Marx wrote in 1853: [12]

> However melancholy we may find the spectacle of the ruin and desolation of these tens of thousands of industrious, peaceful, patriarchal, social groups . . . suddenly cut off from their ancient civilization and their traditional means of existence, we must not forget that these idyllic village communities . . . always provided a firm basis to oriental despotism, confining the human intelligence within the narrowest limits, making of it the obedient traditional instrument of superstition, stunting its growth, robbing it . . . of all capacity of historical activity; let us not forget the egoism of barbarians who, concentrated on an insignificant portion of earth's surface, watched unmoved while immense empires crumbled, unspeakable cruelties were committed, the populations of entire cities were butchered —observed this as if they were events in nature, and so themselves became the helpless victims of every invader who happened to turn his attention to them. . . . In causing social revolution in India, England was, it is true, guided by the lowest motives, and conducted it dully and woodenly. But that is not the point. The question is whether humanity can fulfill its purpose without a complete social revolution in Asia. If not, then England, in spite of all her crimes, was the unconscious instrument of history in bringing about this revolution.

Between the pretensions of nationalism and the ambitions of socialism, the concept of Europe lost much of its former appeal. The great war of 1914–1918 seemed almost a final judgment on a society which had been remarkably reckless in discarding whatever promised to create unity and order. The First World War, by its general excess, created a mood of violence which made itself felt as much in parliaments as on the battlefield. The propaganda of these years exceeded anything which Europe had ever known; each side accused the other of the most abominable intentions and crimes. Any suggestion that the interests of both might be served by a negotiated settlement was dismissed as defeatist or treasonable. Victory was made to appear all-important; in fact, all other benefits were believed to depend on military success.

[12] Quoted in Isaiah Berlin, *Karl Marx* (London: Oxford University Press, 1939), p. 187.

The "saving of Europe," insofar as it was thought of at all, was translated into military terms, each side arguing of course that its victory
would also be Europe's. In these terrifying years, Europe seemed to
show all those qualities which her detractors had always assumed to
be characteristic of her so-called civilization. Belligerence could not
have taken more unpalatable forms; arrogance could not have shown
a more uncompromising character. Europe became involved in a whole
series of enterprises from which she seemed incapable of extricating
herself, enterprises which served only to raise doubts about the intelligence and humanity of those who formulated her policies.

The price of this war was paid in many installments; certain of
the more onerous charges were computed only after the guns were
silenced. The disillusion that set in after the Armistice reflected a failure
not of a single individual but of a social and intellectual process. The
postwar vocabulary, with its heavy emphasis on guilt and retribution,
exploited attitudes which four years of Armageddon had made both
familiar and acceptable. In these circumstances, utopian plans for
Europe's reorganization came principally from men relatively untouched
by such feelings, who in fact had little knowledge of Europe's character,
and cared not at all for her traditional aspirations. This had many dis-
advantages, but in the situation that prevailed nothing else was possible.
Woodrow Wilson and Jan Smuts, more than any European statesmen,
conceived and promulgated the schemes for a better society which
wartime propaganda had promised but had left ambiguous. The League
of Nations—the major political innovation of the period—was constructed
largely from materials and ideas provided by individuals and groups
active in the United States, Great Britain, and in the latter's overseas
Empire. It is not entirely an accident that a volume like Henry Winkler's
The League of Nations Movement in Great Britain, 1914–1919, has
never been written for France.[13] There simply did not exist there or
elsewhere on the Continent an organized sentiment for this sort of
solution to Europe's problems. Wilson and Smuts believed that if
Europe were left to her own devices, there would be an early return
to the aggressive policies of the past. As outsiders, theoretically uncommitted, able to view extreme nationalism dispassionately, they believed
themselves to be particularly well-placed to recommend remedies for
Europe's malady. That such ideas might not appeal to Europeans, or
that they implied an adverse judgment on Europe's earlier history, never

---

[13] Henry R. Winkler, *The League of Nations Movement in Great Britain,
1914–1919* (New Brunswick: Rutgers University Press, 1952); see also, Laurence
W. Martin, *Peace without Victory* (New Haven: Yale University Press, 1958).

occurred to those who were persuaded that Europe was a "lawbreaker," and that only the introduction of competent restraints would prevent a repetition of the tragedy so recently terminated.[14]

The early reaction to the League of Nations, both on the Continent and in Great Britain, was, on the whole, favorable. At one time, in the mid-twenties, the League appeared to enjoy very considerable support. Only after the advent of Hitler did its insufficiencies begin to be commonly recognized. The League seemed incapable either of keeping the peace within Europe or of compelling others outside to do so. Even more serious was the fact that its power to compel member states to accept the responsibilities outlined in the Covenant, particularly in respect to restraining would-be aggressors, seemed severely limited. Europe was incapable of operating the instruments provided her by the Paris peace-makers, and she showed little ingenuity in inventing others more suited to her needs. The idea of creating new political and economic forms, transcending existing national institutions, scarcely entered the arena of political discourse. This was a time for timid and limited gestures; those with utopian visions imagined many things but rarely a united Europe.

The Second World War threw into grim relief the barren topography of these twenty years. From 1939 to 1945, first with only the major West European powers involved, together with Poland, and then, with all except Sweden, Switzerland, Spain and Portugal actually participating, Europe came to know a war as "total" as any the world had ever experienced. Invasion, by land, sea, or air, came to each in turn, with consequences always grave and sometimes tragic. The Second World War, almost from its beginning, assumed a character that made the idea of its being a European "civil war" quite inappropriate. The active participation of "outsiders" was too conspicuous this time; the major battles were fought on and over too many continents and in all the seas of the world. Europe's quarrel became the world's in a way that admitted of no misinterpretation. This was a coming together of many disputes, involving many parties, and not an ingenious gathering of support by Great Britain and France from friends, dependencies and allies beyond the seas. The military operations designed to destroy German power inside Europe, while appearing as primary to those actually suffering the terrors of Nazi occupation, were not, in fact, always as strategically important as those which occurred elsewhere. Reactions to V-E Day expressed perfectly the character of this second

[14] Winston S. Churchill, *The Aftermath* (New York: Scribner, 1929). See particularly his comments on Woodrow Wilson.

great war of the century; for Russia, Norway, Denmark, Belgium and
the peoples of southern and eastern Europe, Germany's defeat constituted the end of hostilities in an effective sense; the French and
Dutch, while equally relieved, accepted the fact that there was still
an enemy to be overcome; the British probably felt this even more
acutely, given the extent of their imperial holdings still under Japanese
occupation, and the Americans understood it in the deepest sense. The
difference in perspective reflected the extent to which the global nature
of the conflict impressed itself on the various belligerents, and this, in
turn, derived from the nature of their individual commitments to others.

While the war was proceeding, few predicted correctly its likely
consequences. The material devastation, by its direct and overpowering
assault on the physical senses, seemed at one time as important as
anything else. The visible damage, in fact, proved to be a relatively
simple matter to repair. While bombs and shells destroyed whole cities
and laid waste great tracts of land, European ingenuity was more than
equal to the task of rapid reconstruction. In this, American aid proved
to be invaluable. It was quite another matter when it came to coping
with the spiritual, moral and human losses. Military casualties, very
heavy for certain of the belligerents, constituted only a part of the
appalling toll. Nazi bestiality sentenced millions to death, and when
Europe learned the full story of this horror, there were no scales adequate to measure the offense. Europe had no experience of such tragedy;
it put into the shade memories of trench warfare in 1914–1918, when
hundreds of thousands fell in vain efforts to gain a few yards of shell-
torn land.[15]

If Europe emerged from the war uncertain about the future, the
reasons were not hard to find. Certainty in this situation would have
been a form of hypocrisy. It was only gradually that indications began
to appear, suggesting what the postwar European world might in fact
be required to contend with. The loss of power—military and political
—seemed obvious. This loss might be remedied in time, but for the
moment the United States and the Soviet Union hovered over Europe
as two colossi, influencing everything—the establishment of new governments, the rate of economic recovery, the stability of particular regimes.

Just as the war bore only a superficial resemblance to what had
happened in 1914–1918, so the post-war period quickly took a course
markedly different from what Europe had known in the 1920's and
1930's. To begin with, there was almost no nostalgia for the immediate

[15] There is no satisfactory study comparing the effects of World War I and
World War II on Europe; this is a great lack.

past. No one thought to go back to "the good old days before 1939"; no one deluded himself that they had been good. More than that, a recognition grew that Europe's situation was in certain respects fundamentally different from any she had known in the past, a fact made immediately inescapable by the presence of Soviet and American military forces. As Europeans reflected on their prospects, they faced first a loss of power, which, in more depressed moments, they chose to translate as a loss of independence. They saw the continent riven by new and unnatural boundaries, expressing the accidents of war more than the circumstances of nationality, history, or geography. Formerly dependent peoples in Asia and Africa rebelled against their European allegiances, or made their intentions so unmistakable that Europeans, occasionally recognizing the advantage of acting quickly, granted independence almost as soon as it was demanded. A structure of relations, carefully built up through the eighteenth and nineteenth centuries, seemed to disintegrate as if it had no substance whatever. In these circumstances, more than sufficient reason existed for concern and even alarm. The extraordinary thing about the postwar period was that neither developed to the extent that might have been predicted. It was as if the war itself had purged Europe of all fears. So much had been experienced—the suffering and loss had been so great—that these new blows fell almost without effect on peoples who had become habituated to adversity. It was as if a whole society wished to skip a generation, forget the shame of two wars,[16] and even more, the disgrace of indecision, weakness and injustice of the first inter-war period, the true "locust years" of the century.

Europeans had every reason to despair, but accepted none of them. While their more remote past appeared almost irrelevant to their new situation, the spirit of enterprise characteristic of those days carried an appeal that caution, which had gone under the name of good sense in more recent times, wholly lacked. There were no Stanley Baldwins about, either in England or elsewhere, dispensing their mild prescriptions for guaranteed safety. This was a blessing. The concept of a single European society, which had gone out of fashion in the second half of the nineteenth century, having become largely the pejorative cliché of non-Europeans, returned to favor. There was no way of knowing how far the revival of European sentiment would go, or what its long-range consequences would be, but there was no denying its reality. Economic

[16] In this matter, an exception must be made for Great Britain. Its recollections of the Second World War, for example, were substantially different from those of occupied and defeated states.

cooperation might stop with the Common Market and never proceed to political union, but this did not alter the fact that the second prospect had been raised in serious political debate throughout Europe, and that it had not been dismissed as visionary. The citizen of Milan, visiting London, came away with a renewed appreciation of the differences between English and Italian society, but the differences seemed less significant than they would have been three decades earlier. No Franco-German understanding could obliterate the distinctive character of each, or entirely cancel out recent history, but the fact that it occurred said something about those who conducted foreign policy in the second postwar era. The French citizen who argued, almost chauvinistically, the importance of language in creating a common civilization, was being no less sincere than the British politician who dwelled on the primary importance of Britain's Commonwealth ties; each, however, lived in a society which understood that these were only partial truths. Increasingly, the idea of Europe penetrated everyone's thinking; men might define the term differently, resist it, but they refused to deny it. A consciousness of Europe, once the property of educated men, became a common possession. As nationality had once won approval from both, so now, the idea of Europe seemed to be a democratic device with its own peculiar attractions.

Geographic proximity, which for so long had seemed the condition of national war and rivalry, emerged as a factor encouraging unity. European frontiers, in the West at least, became demilitarized; the Franco-German understanding was certainly as remarkable a development as any other in a century of diplomatic change. Soviet military power, which loomed ominously at times of crisis, seemed scarcely more threatening to Europeans after 1956 than it did to those more protected by distance. Technology had done much to eradicate the barriers of terrestrial space, and Europeans accepted with a certain stoicism the necessity of living in close proximity to Soviet power. If war came, Europe would almost certainly suffer acutely, but it was not a foregone conclusion that others would suffer less. This was no consolation, obviously, but Europeans had few illusions about what they might themselves do to prevent hostilities. They might try to restrain the Soviets, using argument to recommend caution, and they might employ the same weapon to reason with their American allies. These, however, were means of obviously limited efficacy. The Cuban affair in 1962 told Europeans what they had already guessed—on certain issues involving the security of the United States, Europe would be informed after rather than before the decision-making process was completed, and she would have little to say in what was finally done. It was difficult for any European to believe that a larger control, or even one so large, could ever be maintained over Soviet actions.

European statesmen hurried from conference to conference, flew the oceans of the world, and indicated by their every gesture a continuing interest in maintaining control over their own destinies and in influencing that of others. The incontrovertible reality remained. With severely limited resources, particularly in the military sphere, Europe was incapable of defending herself. This fact could never be lost sight of. Europe's reliance on American protection was total; this situation had no historic parallel. While the Soviet Union and the United States might be concerned with the state of their alliances, their national defense never depended entirely upon alliances being maintained in good repair. Europe was not in anything like the same situation. The connection with America, if impaired, opened at least the possibility of interference by the Soviet Union. The weapons available to Europeans were manifestly insufficient.

This loss of military self-sufficiency coincided with another development, less discussed, but which could prove to be equally important. Europe, for all practical purposes, was excluded from the scientific and technological pursuits associated with the exploration of space. For the first time in centuries major discoveries were taking place in another part of the world, to which Europeans contributed in only the most insignificant manner. All the early steps—including the important ones taken during the Second World War—were enormously indebted to European scientific and technological inventiveness. In the postwar phase, Europe was denied any important share in these activities.

This issue, rarely discussed, symbolized Europe's dilemma. In the pre-1945 world, Europe's centrality, while open to challenge, was never effectively denied. Her citizens succeeded in opening up the world; her ideas dominated in science as well as in the arts; her techniques were studied and copied by all who believed in the possibility of progress. This hegemony was achieved by a society of many states, with large national differences, given to extreme competitiveness, which might take the form of a trade war, but which frequently went beyond and became considerably more hazardous. Others were admitted to European benefits only on condition that they accepted her ways. While there is a danger in making too much of Europe's power before the middle of this century, the greater mistake is to esteem it too low.

Such a dominant position, perhaps, is beyond the capacity of any society today; if so, Europe is simply experiencing what the Americans and Soviets also feel, and what is in any case inevitable, given the facts of modern technology. Dominance once enjoyed, however, is not lightly abandoned, particularly when it seems to define the whole of a society's past experience. A feeling persists in Europe, rarely expressed, that Europe must not simply become the junior partner in a going enterprise, however magnificently managed.[17] Europe's continuing concern is with the possibility of becoming too much the political, intellectual and spiritual disciple of the United States. The opposition to Americanization—which is a sort of short-hand for the complex trends toward modernization—does not derive from underestimating the importance of steel production or the advantages of well-being. Rather, it expresses a sense of the necessity which Europeans feel, that they must continue to be something which Americans are not. This is a strange reversal of roles. Europe, in the twentieth century, is seeking the independence from the other which America so prided itself on securing in the eighteenth. The difficulty of achieving this identity in any meaningful way arises from the fact that there is so little in Europe's recent past that is immediately relevant to the present. The control of vast territories overseas, by economic or political means, is excluded. The destruction of class difference, even where it is more apparent than real, precludes the possibility of maintaining the values characteristic of a more aristocratic society. In the realm of ideas, it is difficult to conceive how Europe can achieve again the sort of primacy that she once enjoyed.

The difficulties of the situation do nothing to diminish or alter the ambition. Consciously or unconsciously, Europe has turned her back on extreme nationalism, imperial rivalry, and military build-up. It is as if the last seven or eight decades have been erased from memory. This, however, does not by itself provide a solution to the problem as it is presently defined. Europe's task is made all the more difficult by the necessity of being reasonable in her criticism of the United States. The freedom to invent clichés about the other—which Americans so much enjoyed in the nineteenth century precisely because no one was listening—is effectively denied Europeans today. It would be taken in bad grace, and, in any case, it would be no solution to Europe's problem. It would not create the distinction that is sought, since it would not be based on any real competence that could be pointed to. Yet, it is precisely this competence that is being sought.

Europe's experience is too deeply and permanently inscribed for illusions to exist about the possibility of starting over again.[18] There

[17] This is not adequately considered by even the better studies on the Atlantic Community.

[18] This is explicitly recognized by the author of one of the best volumes on contemporary Europe, George Lichtheim, *The New Europe* (New York: Praeger, 1963).

may be a "new Europe," but Europe is not a new world. The Flemish will not soon feel differently about the Walloons, though any number of rational arguments may be offered to demonstrate why they should. West Germans will not easily abandon talk of the "unification" of Germany, though many abroad would wish that they might. National pride may be purged of its xenophobic features, but this by itself does not destroy nationalism. Traditional myths and an obsolescent political vocabulary do not disappear simply because they no longer describe a present reality or a future potential. It is in this sense that Europe today, while vastly changed from what she was two and three decades ago, and while prepared to inter that past, is still its victim. Beyond that, there is a longer history with other myths and possibilities which again persist, and which require some sort of modern redefinition. Europe is not ashamed of that past; she instinctively seeks to recreate it.

For the moment, her energy appears to be expended particularly in planning. Cities are being built, industries developed, and agriculture rationalized. Each of these activities creates opportunities and problems. As in the past, politics concerns itself largely with the situations created by immediate developments. Tensions between groups, however defined, continue, and refer back to both long-standing and recent differences. In a relatively static society, education is rarely a problem. In one which is rapidly transforming itself, assuming new directions and developing aspirations which bear only slight resemblance to what was once thought adequate, it becomes a central issue. Funds are obviously required; more that that, there is a pressing need for new ideas. How to educate becomes as controversial as whom to educate. Both are aspects of a dilemma which would not have arisen in the first instance had the society been satisfied or able to remain where it was.

Prophecy is difficult in any century; in the twentieth it appears to be a lost art. No one foresaw in 1953 the Europe of today. There is no reason to believe that a prophecy, registered now about what Europe will be a decade hence, will have any greater validity. This situation is created, in part, by the fact that Europe is not entirely the mistress in her own house. What the United States and the Soviet Union elect to do in the next ten years will influence Europe, and there is only a limited sense in which Europe can determine these actions. More important, however, is the fact that Europe remains undecided about many things and uncertain about what parts of a long and distinguished past can be maintained or revived. As always, she looks at others for comparison and, increasingly, for guidance, but it is not yet clear that she is prepared to be the student of others in the way that Russia was in an earlier day. The abdication by Europe of her own distinctive forms is not easily accepted. If there are no twentieth-century "Slavophils" coming to the fore, reminding Europe of what she had once been, it is because the "Westernizers" remain cautious, and no one recommends complete "Americanization."

Europe's rebuilding and decolonizing tasks have so preoccupied her, have required such vast expenditures of physical and psychic energy, that there has been little incentive to recognize that these were essentially finite operations, which would not indefinitely make important demands on her. In the decade now opening, new preoccupations will undoubtedly assert themselves. More thought, almost certainly, will be given to relations between Western and Eastern Europe. While the Soviet's policy in this matter will be enormously influential, it may be less governing than in the past. Relations between Europe and the states of the Iberian peninsula may change rather dramatically; this "underdeveloped" region of Europe is not necessarily destined to remain so. European-Soviet and European-American relations will almost certainly be modified, in part because of the policies pursued by the great powers, in part because of Europe's own growing consciousness of her own capabilities. It would be hazardous to guess what these changes will be, but it would be wrong to assume that existing relations define what they are likely to be, even in the immediate future. The question of European political unity will certainly continue to be debated. It is not impossible that it will be as unsettled a matter a decade from now as it is today.

For those who are now old, and who have lived their lives in Europe, the century must appear as one of disappointment, with hopes many times raised, only to be finally denied. Neither the liberal nor the socialist utopias have fared well in this century. Nationalism, once thought to have some merit, is now in its extreme forms very properly questioned. If there is an unwillingness to construct new utopias, or to prophesy the certain realization of those now formulated, this reluctance need not be interpreted as evidence of fatigue or skepticism. Europe, by almost any standard that is relevant, shows remarkable vitality and hope. It should not surprise anyone if in the next half century she seeks again, with something approaching her former self-confidence, to be an "example" to the world. The task, while difficult, may be precisely the one to justify the use of that now overworked phrase, the "new Europe." The present efforts, seemingly chaotic, may in time be viewed as the uncertain strivings of an old society to renew itself, by taking what is best from its recollections of a not undistinguished past.

BIBLIOGRAPHY

The following are useful works for beginning the more intensive study of problems raised in the present volume.

Bozeman, Adda B. *Politics and Culture in International History.* Princeton, N. J., Princeton University Press, 1960.

Carr, Edward H. *The Twenty Years Crisis.* London: Macmillan, 1946.

De Visscher, Charles. *Theory and Reality in Public International Law,* translated by P. E. Corbett. Princeton, N. J., Princeton University Center of International Studies. Publications, 1957.

Fischer, Eric. *The Passing of the European Age.* Cambridge, Mass.: Harvard University Press, 1943.

Haas, Ernst B. *The Uniting of Europe.* Stanford, Calif.: London, Stevens & Sons, 1958.

Herz, John. *International Politics in the Atomic Age.* New York: Columbia University Press, 1959.

Hoffmann, Stanley. "International Systems and International Law," *World Politics* **XIV** (1961–1962), pp. 205–37.

———. "International Relations: The Long Road to Theory," *World Politics* **XI** (1958–1959), pp. 347–77.

Holborn, Hajo. *The Political Collapse of Europe.* New York: Alfred Knopf, 1949.

Liska, George. *Nations in Alliance.* Baltimore: The Johns Hopkins Press, 1962.

Mangone, Gerard J. *A Short History of International Organization.* New York: McGraw-Hill, 1954.

Marriott, J. A. R. *Commonwealth or Anarchy: A Survey of Projects of Peace from the Sixteenth to the Twentieth Century.* New York: Oxford University Press, 1939.

Merriam, C. E. *History of the Theory of Sovereignty Since Rousseau.* New York: Columbia College, 1900.

Morgenthau, Hans J. *Politics Among Nations,* Third Edition. New York: Alfred Knopf, 1960.

Vagts, Alfred. "The Balance of Power: Growth of an Idea," *World Politics* **I** (1947–1948), pp. 82–101.

Wolfers, Arnold, and Laurence W. Martin. *The Anglo-American Tradition in Foreign Affairs.* New Haven, Conn.: Yale University Press, 1956.